POSSIBLE

"**Success is POSSIBLE, not just a distant dream.** The Success Pledge is a powerful, transformative roadmap that can guide you toward your goals and dreams. Are you prepared to embark on your journey to success? Judge Elijah Smiley shares his personal story to show how adhering to the Success Pledge can pave the way for success. The Success Pledge is presented as a potent blueprint for success, with readers being carefully guided through its practical implementation, fostering a sense of hope and optimism for a prosperous future."

COVER PHOTO-1995
(Judge Elijah Smiley, and wife, Kathy, and Chief Judge Don Sirmons and Florida Governor Lawton Chiles)

POSSIBLE

Unleash Your Imagination Without Limits

JUDGE ELIJAH SMILEY, J.D., M.B.A., C.P.A.,
A DISTINGUISHED PROFESSIONAL
WITH A WEALTH OF EXPERIENCE AND
KNOWLEDGE.

This introspective memoir provides a detailed account of the author's vivid recollections from various pivotal experiences throughout his life. Certain events have been thoughtfully condensed to capture their essence, while select dialogues have been meticulously recreated to bring the narrative to life. All rights to this evocative and deeply personal account are reserved.

ISBN: 979-8-9913368-0-2 (Paperback)
ISBN: 979-8-9913368-1-9 (Hardcover)
ISBN: 979-8-9913368-2-6 (eBook)

Library of Congress Control Number: 2024917465

DEDICATION

This book is dedicated to my wife, Kathy, and daughter, Danielle, as well as my dear friends Keith and Joyce Blanden of Waxhaw, North Carolina. I also dedicate this to Reverend Jarvis Bracy, Sr., who passed on June 17, 2022, his wife Vanessa, and their children Aaron and Arielle of Jacksonville, Florida.

ACKNOWLEDGMENTS

I thank God for his abundant blessings, provisions, and protection. I am indebted to my family, church, and community for their steadfast support—a special thanks to Darlene Cutler, my Judicial Assistant for 20 years. I thank Dr. Cheryl Jennings, President of SokheChapke Publishing, for her invaluable contributions.

YOU CAN MAKE A DIFFERENCE. IT DOESN'T TAKE MUCH.

Your actions, no matter how small, can significantly impact your community. You have the power to make a positive difference.

God has given us the gifts of hope, charity, and love.

Each of us has a significant role in making our community a better place for our children. God has given us the gifts of love, hope, and charity. I encourage you to fan into flame your gifts. It doesn't take much to make a difference. A small act of kindness or a word of encouragement may be the catalyst that inspires strength, love, and self-discipline in our youth or cause some young person to reach new heights and strive for a better and brighter tomorrow.

I hope you will strive for excellence in all your endeavors and become a shining example of kindness, generosity, and hope for our young people who may one day follow in our footsteps. You have the power to make a difference. What are you doing to make a positive difference?

BE A DIFFERENCE-MAKER IN YOUR COMMUNITY

Many Blessings,
Judge Elijah, Kathy, and Danielle Smiley

CONTENTS

THE SUCCESS
PLEDGE

- SET CLEAR GOALS

- WORK HARD TO REACH

  YOUR GOALS

- MAKE GOOD CHOICES

- BELIEVE IN YOURSELF &

  NEVER GIVE UP!

I CAN AND I WILL
REACH MY GOALS

INTRODUCTION:
THE SUCCESS PLEDGE

It is the most incredible time in the history of the world to be alive. We have more freedom and opportunity than ever, and the future holds even more promise. Impossible opportunities are now possible. Fundamental rights that were once beyond our reach are now at our doorsteps. The unequal circumstances in history that denied our ancestors the chance to excel can no longer hold our dreams and ambitions captive. A few generations ago, legal, structural, and social barriers made it impossible for my parents to vote, obtain a formal education, or achieve their highest potential. However, within their lifetimes, their aspirations, dreams, and hopes have finally been realized through their children and grandchildren. There are no longer impossible odds or barriers that one cannot conquer. Our young people must utilize all their gifts and talents to reach their goals. They should grab the chance to rise above the odds, especially if they are curious and eager to learn, because they represent our best hope for tomorrow. Likewise, we must put forth our best effort to help guide, nurture, and equip them to succeed.

Success means doing your absolute best by using your God-given talents, whatever they may be, to unlock your fullest potential. Thanks be to God; only *you* can shackle or unshackle your mind. You and only you determine whether you are doing your best. The possibilities are endless and are as great as you make them. I appeal to you to remove any limitations on your imagination because there *are* no limitations. Imagine the impossible and make it happen. Dr. Mae Jemison, an engineer, physician, and astronaut, was the first African American woman in space. She famously said, "Never be limited by other people's limited imaginations." That message rings true for anyone who desires to achieve their dreams.

No matter what stage of life you are in, you can positively impact the future. There's nothing too good that you cannot achieve, and there are no obstacles too high or too deep for you to rise above if you set your sights high. Stay focused on your goals and work hard to achieve success.

I proudly share my life story and a snapshot of the history of my hometown, Port St. Joe, Florida, because achieving success is possible. How your family raises you and those influencing you can profoundly impact who you eventually become. This belief has always resonated with me personally and professionally over time.

In the years before I went off to college at Florida State University, I dreamed of my destined future. I dreamed of what was indeed POSSIBLE. I did not dwell on the challenges that could (or might) have held me down. Instead, I imagined the forthcoming possibilities. I imagined what I wanted to achieve and what I needed to do to attain the rewards of my efforts. An unwavering commitment to hard work and the love and support from my family, friends, and community bolstered my desire to reach my goals. The fulfillment of my dreams came to fruition because I focused on putting the principles of the Success Pledge into daily action.

The Key components of the Success Pledge are:

1. Setting Clear Goals

2. Working Hard to Reach Your Goals

3. Making Good Choices Using Your Faith and Family Training as a Guide

4. Believing in Yourself and Never Giving UP!

I will guide you through implementing the success pledge in Chapter 8. The success pledge principles form the very foundation of my career and have significantly contributed to my accomplishments. I confidently offer this pledge as a powerful guide for you or someone you know to achieve their desired goals.

Chapter 1
BEGINNINGS ALONG THE WAY: THE FIRST INFLUENCERS IN MY LIFE

"Every child should be as fortunate as I was to have reaped the benefits of learning from so many supportive and self-sacrificing educators."

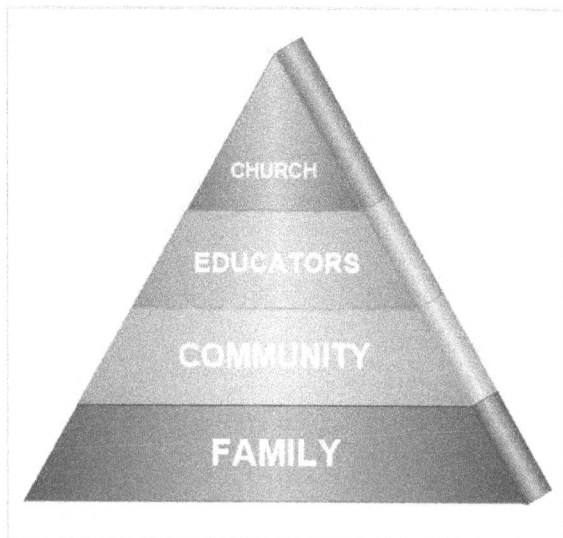

Our journey in life has a beginning and an end. Within the journey, countless events touch us in ways that shape who we are. There is no question that every decision we make during the journey can fundamentally change us for a lifetime. This transformative power of personal choices is what empowers us. Time and time again, our behavior has been proven to define us in the long run. Because of this, *character* matters. How we conduct ourselves matters. What we do and say reflects who we are and who we may become. The point here is that we may never know how our conduct and actions impact others. For example, a young person beginning her path in life may get inspired by someone for various reasons, good or bad. Therefore, we should always try to help others unlock the wealth of opportunities awaiting them.

My successes and achievements thus far have been made POSSIBLE by the guidance, support, and inspiration provided by a remarkable network of individuals who have selflessly invested in my journey. From the nurturing encouragement of my family to the nurturing mentorship of dedicated educators and the wisdom imparted by religious and community leaders, each has played a pivotal role in shaping my path. Their collective influence has propelled me to a successful career while instilling a deep sense of gratitude and a commitment to paying it forward in my endeavors.

My Family

Throughout my life, I have valued my immediate and extended community family beyond measure. Having a loving family was especially important as I grew up in North Port St. Joe, Florida, where neighbors and friends cared deeply about the well-being of every child. My parents, aunts, uncles, cousins, ministers, and teachers have been a constant source of inspiration and guidance throughout my career. Growing up with my siblings, our parents loved us unconditionally. They fostered a caring environment and encouraged us to become our best selves. In a home where moral standards were virtuous, my mother and father expected us to pursue the best education imaginable, one that would give us a good quality of life. Reading books of interest, completing homework, participating in our church community, and being responsible for household chores instilled habits of responsibility and accountability in us. Our modest home was a place of open communication where we learned from countless exemplars our mother and father set forth. I learned some of the best examples of the work ethic principle found in my *success pledge* from my father, observing him as a 25-year laborer at St. Joe Paper Mill, and my mother, a homemaker. Not once did I see my parents show ill will toward anyone. From them, we all learned to treat every person with utmost respect and kindness. A meaningful life lesson taught by our parents was to live life honestly while striving to have a good impact on others and, therefore, make a difference in the world. These principles of human decency and goodwill extended beyond the home into church, school, and daily encounters.

Educators

Every child should be as fortunate as I was to have reaped the benefits of learning from so many supportive and self-sac-rificing educators. I have fond memories of my elementary school teachers, including Christine Williams (first grade), Ruth Phillips (fourth grade), and CoJean Burns (sixth grade), who were equally attentive to every student. I still remember my father bringing bananas and snacks to Mrs. Phillips' class for my lunch breaks. The enthusiasm these teachers had for enriching the minds of young children was a heartwarming display of professionalism. They welcomed curious learners into their classrooms, frequently engaged in parent-teacher meetings, attended extracurricular events, and consistently modeled positive character while prepar-ing every child to be a successful learner. My high school teachers, Clarence Monette, Christine and Carl White, Lin-da Kent, and former High School Principal Edwin Williams, were remarkable examples of great educators. The impres-sions they made on me as a youth were intrinsically worth-while. They exemplified a thirst for knowledge inside and outside their classrooms. I recall stimulating discussions that stirred my interest in seeking deeper meanings and under-standings of issues impacting our society then.

Since my grade school and college years, I have come to understand that teachers can be the catalyst that can effec-tively change the direction of a student's life. Beyond doubt, great teachers can instill excitement for learning in their students, particularly young people who don't always recognize what a good education might afford them. I experienced the confidence of such great teachers throughout my education, and it is a testament to the transformative power of education that can inspire and bring hope to all.

Mr. Clarence Monette, the admired Port St. Joe High School Librarian/Media Specialist, was an integral part of the Port St. Joe community and a captivating teacher. I recall afternoons at the end of the school day, finding my way through aisles and aisles of books on every subject that any young person might want to know more about. He was always there to answer questions provoked by displays of popular books or postings on bulletin boards containing school notices on topics of interest. His passion for teaching about the world galvanized my desire to continue my education. Many years after I graduated from High School, Mr. Monette continued his long-standing legacy of stimulating students' curiosity. In later years, when I assumed the role of Circuit Judge, I had the privilege of addressing students at the Port St. Joe High School Black History Month event in 2002. Also, I had the opportunity to visit the Port St. Joe High School library. Returning to my old school as a guest speaker was an emotionally significant and rewarding experience in my professional journey. The genuine curiosity and engagement of the students regarding my work filled me with hometown pride. Thanks to Mr. Monette, long before the Google age, books in the school library were often the only means of venturing outside of Gulf County through reading. While today, the information medium may be different and dominated by the digital age, libraries still serve a valuable purpose for inciting learning. What young people from my generation sought in their dreams was often found in the books on Mr. Monette's library shelves. I kept my library card for years, knowing it was a literary ticket to places unknown and places I would eventually see one day. Mr. Monette and the other teachers in Port St. Joe embodied how character matters and how the impact of a good character goes a long way.

Port St. Joe Community & Religious Leaders

Reverend Charles P. Price's remarkable character firmly distinguished him from others. He was a giant of a man, both intellectually and spiritually. He was born in the 1890s in Georgia, where he remained until his early teens. By age 14, he ended up in the Gulf Coast town of Apalachicola, a bustling fishing town in Franklin County, Florida, just twenty-three miles from Port St. Joe. He moved there with his mother and siblings, seeking better opportunities and decent jobs in the panhandle region, as many Black families did during that time. In due time, Reverend Price would eventually make his way to Port St. Joe, Florida.

It is fair to say that the entire Port St. Joe community admired Charles P. Price, affectionately known as the Pastor of Zion Fair Missionary Baptist Church. The church, originally named Zion Fair Colored Missionary Baptist Church, is a historic building over a century old and is still an integral part of North Port St. Joe. In 1974, the word 'Colored,' referencing the race of its membership, was removed from the church name. Pastor Price was an esteemed individual who made a lasting impression on everyone. He had an abiding concern and sincere care for his congregation. He also had an uncanny knack for dispensing advice and spiritual counseling to anyone who sought it, often using examples from his infinite wisdom.

When I was a teen in the early seventies, it was not unusual to see Reverend Price sitting on the porch of the old white wooden parsonage next to the Church on Avenue C in Port St Joe. One would typically see him wearing a stiffly pressed white shirt and a perfectly knotted tie. His poised demeanor conveyed dignity and self-assurance.

Admiration for Reverend Price resulted from his countless contributions to the betterment of North Port St. Joe. As a model of community leadership, Reverend Price was beyond comparison. He likely developed his disciplined and committed leadership style from his family upbringing and a brief stint in the U.S. Army; he was one of the few Black men from our area who served in WWI. He later followed his Christian Leadership ambitions and became a licensed and ordained minister. His active ministry played a pivotal role in community affairs as he worked to improve race relations in Gulf County. He exuded wisdom, knowledge, and a kindness of spirit toward parishioners that was second to none. He was also known to be unassuming, humble, and consistently respectful. Unsurprisingly, I wanted to follow the example of his reputable character and desired to be just like him. Reverend Price would remain in the panhandle region for the rest of his life. When he passed away in 1981, it was a significant loss to all who knew him. A quote from the church's website confirms Pastor Price's dedication to his parishioners: "Zion Fair has been a guiding light for many Christians throughout the years. Many have been inspired and encouraged to continue in the work of the Lord. Many young people have been equipped with the character and moral foundation to achieve great success."

Similarly, other esteemed area community members made a profoundly positive impact on me. For example, Reverend Henry C. McCray, moderator of the New Gulf Coast Baptist Association; Reverend Jackson E. Jones, long time Pastor of Panama City St. John Missionary Baptist Church and NAACP leader; and Reverend Otis Stallworth, Pastor of Port St. Joe Church of God In Christ and the grocery store owner in Port St. Joe, Florida, were well-regarded. They may never have realized how their influence helped guide me toward my goals. Throughout my personal and professional life, I have tried my best to come close to the qualities exhibited by Reverend Price and others whom I deeply admired.

Individuals possessing a wide range of talents, experiences, and knowledge are invaluable today. To advance and develop, it is crucial to approach the wise advice others offer with humility and respect. I once said, *"It's not where you start; it's where you end up."* This point is undoubtedly valid, but family and community are foundational in shaping good character. Our character embodies who each of us becomes. It has been a joy and privilege to receive so much goodwill, guidance, and prayers from my family, church, and community. For these reasons, whatever small amount that I may have achieved is attributed to God and to those whom God, in his infinite wisdom, has allowed to be a part of my journey along the way.

Chapter 2
MY EARLY JOURNEY – 1950S AND 1960S

"There is something unmistakably good about the sacrifices of military service, and those who commit to serve do so with the most incredible honor. I was only ten when Congressional Medal of Honor Recipient SSG Clifford Sims was ceremoniously laid to rest in our hometown at Zion Fair Missionary Baptist Church."

Port St. Joe, Florida Papermill 1938-1999

A Glimpse at Early PSJ History and the 1950s

My life began in Gulf County, Florida, a small but stunningly beautiful part of our vast nation. Gulf County's largest city, Port St. Joe, is the seat of official county government business. The Courthouse is one of our well-known landmarks on the edge of town. Port St. Joe is located on the white sandy edges of the Gulf of Mexico, the largest Gulf in the world. I was blessed to be born here. It is where you can walk along pristine beaches just minutes from the doorsteps of my original home. It is also where my family has lived for nearly a century.

It is worth noting that Port St. Joe has a fascinating history, witnessed in part by my ancestors who came before me. Known initially as St. Joseph and established in 1835 as a seaport, it was ideal for shipping cargo to various parts of the country. The town's thriving economy earned attention in 1837 as it grew to become the largest city in the state, with a population of more than 12,000. The following year, in 1838, Florida's first Constitution was written in St. Joseph, paving the way for Florida to become the 27th state in the Union on March 3, 1845, when President John Tyler signed an Act of Admission. A museum commemorating this event in Florida's history is minutes from where I grew up. I was reminded of the significance of this historic site to the state and my hometown each time I passed it on my way to high school.

As a native, I am incredibly familiar with the various weather conditions that impact people living near the Gulf of Mexico. History reveals that in the 1800s, natural disasters and human missteps diminished the economic vitality of St. Joseph. There was a destructive fire that engulfed the town in 1841, while at about the same time, a Yellow Fever epidemic claimed countless lives regardless of status, ethnicity, or race. The quick spreading viral disease was feared, so much so that victims were buried in a cemetery apart from others; the site where victims were ostracized remains there today. Additionally, the city maintains public but separate cemeteries for whites and Black Americans–Holly Hill Cemetery for whites and Forest Hill for Black people. Although it was an accepted tradition of the past, it remains a remnant of a once racially divided community.

However, the town's quick downfall did not stop with a few tragic events in its early history. Fewer than three years after the epidemic and fire, two hurricanes of epic proportions in 1843 and 1851 wreaked havoc in the Panhandle region of Florida, destroying St. Joseph's economic infrastructure, including the railroad and other shipping-related industries. The impact of two hurricanes on the economy irreversibly forced shipping and rail-supported commerce into bankruptcy. As the once vibrant economy declined, so did the town's population, with historical records indicating that no more than five hundred residents remained by 1842. Fortunately, my ancestors had not yet established themselves in Port St. Joe, and none of our relatives perished due to these unfortunate events. In time, my ancestors would make their way to the Panhandle of Florida in the ensuing years. Once there, they demonstrated resilience despite unexpected and unforeseen obstacles. My family's predecessors laid the foundation for a path of opportunity that began in slavery one hundred years before I was born.

My Family History, Family Tree (grandparents, parents)

My *great-grandparents* were born into slavery in the 1850s, a time when the Civil War had yet to occur, nor had the United States Supreme Court decided the Dred Scott case in 1857. Scott was an incredibly courageous Black man who challenged the law of the land at that time. In Dred Scott v. Sandford (argued in 1856 and decided in 1857), the Supreme Court ruled, after weeks of contentious debate, that Americans of African descent, whether a free or enslaved person, were not American citizens and could not sue in federal court. The Court also ruled that Congress lacked the power to ban slavery in the U.S. territories. Finally, the Court declared that the Fifth Amendment constitutionally protected the rights of enslavers because enslaved people were categorized as property. Under the law of the land, the United States Supreme Court identified my great-grandparents as mere property worthy of no protected rights. This historic ruling was a devastating blow to over ten thousand enslaved people.

When my **grandparents** were born in the 1870s and 1880s, during the Reconstruction Era, the Union had recently prevailed in the Civil War between the states, and the 13th, 14th, and 15th Amendments to the United States Constitution were only enacted a decade earlier.

My grandmother, Colorado Wynn-Roulhac (standing), was born in 1887 in Jackson County, Florida. She is pictured here with her siblings, George, Plassett, and Calvin Wynn. Their experiences, struggles, and triumphs are a testament to the resilience and determination that runs through our family history, and their stories continue to inspire me.

After the Civil War, **the 13th Amendment** to the U.S. Constitution was officially ratified in 1865. This crucial amendment dictates that:

"Neither slavery nor involuntary servitude, except as a punishment for the crime of which the party shall have been duly convicted, shall exist within the United States, or any place subject to their jurisdiction."

The 13th Amendment marked the official end of slavery in the United States, and it effectively nullified the 1857 United States Supreme Court Dred Scott ruling that had previously upheld slavery. This monumental step towards justice and equality reshaped history for my family and countless others, including my grandparents, whose lives were profoundly affected by this historic change.

The 14th Amendment to the United States Constitution, officially adopted on July 9, 1868, holds immense historical significance as one of the three Reconstruction Amendments following the Civil War. It introduced a transformative change by granting citizenship to all individuals "born or naturalized in the United States." This inclusive provision was especially meaningful for those previously enslaved and represented a monumental step towards national unity and equality. In addition, the amendment sought to establish the principle of "equal protection under the laws," thereby extending the fundamental safeguards outlined in the Bill of Rights to every citizen within the states. My esteemed grandparents, Preston and Irene Smiley and Isacc and Colorada Roulhac represented the venerated pioneers in my family lineage who were among the earliest recipients of the legal entitlement to citizenship as conferred by the 14th Amendment. Their experiences stand as a testament to the enduring impact of this landmark constitutional provision.

On February 3, 1870, **the 15th Amendment** to the United States Constitution was ratified, granting all citizens the right to vote regardless of race, color, or previous condition of servitude. However, despite this guarantee, it would be another hundred years before my family lineage could exercise this right. My parents were born in the early 1900s, just a few years after the United States Supreme Court, in the landmark Plessy v. Ferguson (1896) case, upheld the constitutionality of racial segregation laws for public facilities as long as the segregated facilities were deemed "separate but equal." This ruling perpetuated racial inequality and hindered the full realization of civil rights for Black Americans. This doctrine came to be known as "separate but equal." This period, which followed the end of the Reconstruction Era (1865–1877), was a tough time for my grandparents. They were extraordinary, ordinary folks who did not have the opportunity to think about education or accumulating wealth; they just wanted to work and improve things for their children.

Like many Black people from Alabama, my father, Joe Smiley, moved to Port St. Joe in the '40s to pursue work at the St. Joe Paper Company. My mother, Pecola Smiley, moved from a small town called Campbellton in neighboring Jackson County, Florida. My father's relocation to Florida was tied to what historians call the Great Migration (circa 1915) and the Second Great Migration from Alabama (1942-1945), where Black people were moving north in record numbers to escape the hardships attached to Jim Crow laws and to places where they found racial tolerance and greater freedom. While many followed the northern path, my father made a different choice. He decided to leave behind a future in cotton sharecropping in Alabama and found work at the St. Joe Paper Mill, which produced paper from wood, pulp, and other ingredients.

As was the case for most Black people then, his lack of a formal education roadblocked higher wages and employment that would have paid more. So, getting employment at the mill was a blessing. Founded in 1936 by Edward Ball, a politically influential man in Florida for many decades, the St. Joe Mill and Box Plant boosted the local economy. Mr. Ball spearheaded the St. Joe Paper Company with the help of the Alfred du Pont Testamentary Trust. Ball collaborated with the *Pork Chop Gang*- a powerful Florida Democrat group- to buy cheap land in the Florida Panhandle. The investors accrued enormous wealth from the land boom.

My father, the chief breadwinner, and my mother gave us a masterful example of pursuing personal fulfillment. It was simple: work hard and treat others with respect and kindness. They also expected us to beat the odds and become productive citizens despite obstacles. They wanted us to make something of ourselves. All of us met the challenge and went on to become productive citizens.

Working long hours at the paper mill was not the only avenue Black people in Port St. Joe followed to improve their livelihood. Serving in the United States military was another route many young people in Port St. Joe chose after graduating high school. Joining the Army or other branches of the armed forces was a prideful decision. For some, the military ensured lifelong benefits, including advanced education. For others, it was their best chance to see the world. Almost everyone from the small North Port St. Joe community has a family member or knows someone who served in the military.

African Americans' military history dates from their arrival on U.S. shores as enslaved Africans during the colonial period to the present day. African Americans have participated in every war fought by or within the United States, including the Revolutionary War, the War of 1812, the Mexican-American War, the Civil War, the Spanish-American War, World War I, World War II, the Korean War, the Vietnam War, the Gulf War, the War in Afghanistan, and the Iraq War. Citizens of North Port St. Joe have served in every war since World War I. Those I've known to have served in the military include siblings, uncles, nephews, nieces, cousins, close friends, and neighbors. My uncles, Charlie Roulhac and Humor Roulhac, and my cousins, Henry Wynn, Charlie Wynn, and Robert Williams, all served in World War II. Several of my siblings served in the military: Isacc served in Vietnam, Mitchell Smiley retired from the United States Army, and Anita Tiller served in the National Guard. Many of my nephews, cousins, and friends also served loyally to protect the freedom, liberty, and pursuit of happiness granted by the Constitution and bestowed by God.

As a native of North Port St. Joe, I can easily underscore the belief that patriotism runs deep and wide in the North Port St. Joe enclave. Port St. Joe natives' pride for and loyalty to the United States have endured for generations, with some individuals being honored with the nation's highest accolades for commendable service. The Medal of Honor is the highest military decoration awarded by the U.S. government. The President bestows it in the name of Congress. It is conferred only upon members of the United States Armed Forces who distinguish themselves through "conspicuous gallantry and intrepidity at the risk of his or her life above and beyond the call of duty while engaged in an action against an enemy of the United States."

It is worth noting that the Congressional Medal of Honor recipient SSG Clifford Chester Sims, who gave his life in defense of American liberty bequeathed to us by God, was born and spent his youthful years on the familiar streets in North Port St. Joe. Sims was leading a squad near Hue, Vietnam when they were hit by enemy fire. He led his men in an attack to free a platoon pinned down and then provided covering fire. After moving no more than thirty meters, Sims noticed that a building holding ammunition was on fire. He quickly moved his squad, limiting serious casualties to two men. While continuing through the dense woods amid heavy enemy fire, Sims heard the trigger of a concealed booby trap to their front. He hurled himself upon the device, sacrificing his life. SSG Sims, who had distinguished himself as a skilled leader, made the ultimate sacrifice during the Vietnam conflict on February 21, 1968. His selfless action spared the lives of countless fellow soldiers. On March 15, 1968, at 10:00 a.m., the funeral service for Congressional Medal of Honor Recipient SSG Clifford Sims was held at Zion Fair Missionary Baptist Church in Port St. Joe, Florida. The following year, Vice President of the United States, Spiro Agnew, presented SSG Sim's distinguished medal posthumously to his family on December 2, 1969, in Washington, D.C. As a show of community pride, the North Port St. Joe Veterans Monument was erected to preserve the incontestable valor for years in recognition of SSG Sims and more than three hundred other veterans, including Command Sergeant Major Sidney Weatherspoon, who received the Legion of Merit and Bronze Star for exceptionally meritorious conduct during armed conflict, and Colonel Dorothy Mount Austin, the highest-ranking woman military officer from North Port St. Joe. There is something unmistakably good about the sacrifices of military service, and those who commit to serve do so with the most incredible honor. I was only ten when Congressional Medal of Honor Recipient SSG Clifford Sims was ceremoniously laid to rest in our hometown at Zion Fair Missionary Baptist Church.

The next generation of Smileys

Some extraordinary events marked the late 1950s, and the Civil Rights Movement was chief among them. When I was born on November 6, 1959, at the Gulf Pines Hospital in Port

St. Joe, Florida, to Joe and Pecola Smiley, I was blessed to be a part of the Smiley lineage. I am the tenth of eleven siblings (six brothers and four sisters) born in the middle of the modern Civil Rights Era. I was born five years after the United States Supreme Court decision in the landmark case *Brown v. Board of Education* (1954), which declared that the *Plessy v Ferguson* (1896) "separate but equal" doctrine violated the 14th Amendment and that segregating children by race in public schools was "inherently unequal." Ultimately, the Brown decision led to the integration of public schools across the nation and in Gulf County. The winds of change were boldly blowing when I was born.

Early childhood dreams (grade school friends)

As a child, I remember eating meals at the family dinner table while listening to my parents talk about their dreams for their children. Stories about what it was like growing up in Alabama and working long hours on cotton farmland that didn't belong to him or his family. Initially, I had little curiosity about places far away from my safe and close-knit family, as my attention was mainly on church and school attendance. I also did not think much about human conditions and cultures outside our small town because North Port St. Joe was my entire world. However, my view of the world changed as I entered my junior high years and started mindfully devising my goals.

In the close-knit community of North Port St. Joe, there was a deep-rooted commitment to instill traditional values of respect, responsibility, and integrity in the upbringing of its children. The village took great pride in upholding these principles, ensuring the younger generation was nurtured in an environment that celebrated honorable conduct and moral fortitude. Our grade-school teachers and parents collaborated to instill virtuous habits, set high academic expectations, and inspire greatness in each of us. This strong community support, discipline, and constant care kept us on the right path, with only a few young people faltering along the way. I later learned that the world was considerably larger than Port St. Joe, and events affected us even if we didn't know it then. For instance, two years before I was born, many important events, including the Civil Rights Act of 1957, set the stage for my future. The Civil Rights Act of 1957 was established to ensure voting rights for all American Citizens and was the first Civil Rights legislation enacted by Congress since Reconstruction. The same year, the Soviets launched Sputnik, ushering in many subsequent decades of competition between the United States and Russia, mainly to be the first in space. Alaska and Hawaii became our 49th and 50th states in the year I was born. It was also the period when the enforcement of the Brown vs the Board of Education decision encountered resistance, and it was when the first nine black students integrated into a school in Arkansas had to be protected by the United States 101 Airborne, as ordered by President Eisenhower, to ensure their safety.

It was a time when conflicts in Civil Rights matters were reaching a boiling point. I was just a year old in 1960 when the Greensboro Sit-ins ignited. Four Black college students, with unwavering courage, took a stand at a segregated lunch counter, igniting a wave of protests. Soon after, the Nashville Sit-in inspired other students to join in similar peaceful demonstrations across the nation. These bold and unprecedented acts of bravery by young people sent a resounding message to America. Similarly, Harper Lee's bestselling book *To Kill a Mockingbird*, published in 1960, vividly portrayed the harsh realities of living in the Jim Crow South in Alabama in the 1930s. These were the realities of those like my father, born in 1901 in Alabama. The book presents the compelling story of racism, moral courage, and the power of innocence that has influenced several generations' ideas about justice, race relations, and poverty. Lead character Atticus Finch expressed the ideal vision of our court system when he said, *"But there is one way in this country in which all men are created equal—there is one human institution that makes a pauper the equal of a Rockefeller, the stupid man the equal of an Einstein, and the ignorant man the equal of any college president. That institution, gentlemen, is a court. It can be the Supreme Court of the United States or the humblest J.P. court in the land, or this honorable court which you serve. Our courts have their faults, as does any human institution, but in this country our courts are the great levelers, and in our courts all men are created equal."*

At the same time, many important events occurring around the globe in the first years of my life added clarity to my future direction for decades to come. To list a few, the Vietnam War started in 1960 at a time when North Port St. Joe residents served the nation in the armed forces; John Glenn orbited the earth in 1962; and Dr. Martin Luther King, Jr., delivered his "I Have a Dream" speech in 1963, the centenary year of the Emancipation Proclamation, in which then-President Abraham Lincoln had freed the enslaved Africans in the United States in 1863. In his speech, Dr. King praised the 'magnificent words' of the US Constitution and the Declaration of Independence, highlighting their role in the Civil Rights movement. He reminded us that his dream is 'deeply rooted' in the American Dream: that notion that anybody, regardless of their background, can become prosperous and successful in the United States. He dreamed of the day that the children of America would be judged not by the color of their skin but by the content of their character. It is up to us to make the dream of equality and justice under the Constitution real for every citizen.

In the pivotal year of 1963, the United States suffered the devastating losses of President John F. Kennedy and Civil Rights activist Medgar Evers. Both were tragically assassinated within months of each other. Within five years of these two tragic events, Dr. Martin Luther King, Jr. was assassinated in 1968.

President Lyndon B. Johnson, President Kennedy's Vice President, eventually proposed the historically acclaimed Great Society, which called for societal reforms to dismantle national poverty and discrimination. President Johnson's Great Society was implemented through educational and medical improvement programs. Johnson also nominated Thurgood Marshall as the first African American to the United States Supreme Court. All these noteworthy milestones in the first ten years of my life proved that anything is possible and that the future is typically fashioned by those who have effectively applied the principles of the success pledge. While I was too young to grasp these history-making events as they unfolded, I would later appreciate their relevance in my life, especially as an attorney and judge.

Chapter 3
THE 1970S: TEENAGE YEARS

"Typically, up and ready to go at 5:00 a.m. on weekend mornings, I would get on my 1975 350cc red Honda motorcycle and head to the St. Joseph Bay Country Club to wash golf carts. The Country Club was about ten miles away by motorcycle from where I lived in North Port St Joe."

I was self-motivated to do well and had an exceptional grade school experience. While it sometimes required extra effort to succeed in certain classes, I only recall a few challenges. The years on the honor roll were earned with tremendous pride. I persevered in my studies, wanting to reap the highest marks in every subject. Near my tenth birthday, events of epic proportions happened around the time I reached fifth and sixth grade. Expectedly, Mr. Monette, the school's librarian, opened our eyes to them. In 1969, for instance, Apollo 11 Astronauts Neil Armstrong and Buzz Aldrin landed and bravely walked on the moon, a monumental achievement in human history that inspired me to reach for the stars in my life. At the same time, world-famous Maya Angelou, an African American poet, published 'I Know Why the Caged Bird Sings,' a book that resonated with me and many others, sparking meaningful conversations about race and identity. And even though it was unimaginable to have computers readily available, the floppy disk, a predecessor of the USB drive, was invented by IBM. A while later, in 1976, Steve Jobs introduced the world to Apple Computer. The science of and fascination with computing technology would evolve quickly in the following decades. So, these milestones made school relevant and meaningful to us students. Plus, I had no desire to disappoint my parents and family, who had made many sacrifices for me. Besides, my parents were not strangers to the rudiments of parental involvement. It was customary for them to push us to be our very best. In all, they expected my siblings and I to be good stewards of the Smiley name.

Christian Values and High Expectations

My father was genuinely kindhearted but also a firm disciplinarian. He believed in the principle of fairness for everyone. His strong family values prevailed. My destiny was influenced early by my hard-working father and my mother's example, who pushed us to do nothing less than our best. They instilled a strong work ethic and a sense of responsibility that guided me through my academic journey. His sense of justice and patience as a father and provider gave me insights into my role as a future parent, lawyer, and judge. His examples of fatherhood guided my abilities to apply justice from the bench. He truly believed that every person should be accountable for their actions regardless of status.

Community churches and Sunday Schools were filled with young people in the early seventies. Attending a church for most youth was a community norm and expectation. Practically everyone attended church in our home, as did everyone else in North Port St. Joe. Most of our neighbors shared the same routines of going to school, working at the St. Joe Mill, and attending church. Growing up, I had many active roles at Zion Fair Missionary Baptist Church. I learned valuable life lessons about leadership from my church family, where I served as youth president and Sunday School Secretary as a teen. These experiences helped me develop organizational skills, public speaking abilities, and the ability to collaborate with others. To this day, I treasure my award for winning the New Gulf Coast Baptist Student Oratorical Contest in 1975, held at New Bethel Baptist Church in Panama City, Florida. I participated in many celebrations at church, including Easter and Christmas programs. I also looked forward to regional and state church associations every year. Since my early youth and to this day, my Christian beliefs have been integral to my life experiences and being a contributing member of my community.

Fully Integrated Public Schools in Gulf County

Remember, by the time I was born in 1959, Brown v. the Board of Education had already been signed into law, and a change in educational access was coming. Before this historic decision, the idea of the 'separate but equal' practice was still applied. Although slow to be fully integrated, school systems in the South reluctantly began the complex task of changing the face of classrooms, where Black and white children engaged in cohabited learning for the first time in United States history. My parents, who grew up in the pre-Civil Rights era, were not blessed with the good fortune of a grade-school education, and my older siblings were, too, subjected to "segregated by race "classrooms from kindergarten through 12th grade in the all-black George Washington School. Then, school integration was put into play.

Judge Smiley attended George Washington Elementary School, Port St Joe, Florida, built in the 1940s.

Initially, a small portion of the town's Black student population enrolled in Port St. Joe High School. My siblings, Willie Mae Harris(record-holding all-star basketball player), Robert Farmer, Ruby Farmer, Versa McCloud, Isacc Farmer, Willie Smiley, and Mitchel Smiley, spent their entire grade school years at George Washington School, built in 1940 to serve as the school facility for Black students in the first through twelfth grades. However, Joseph Smiley, Anita Smiley, Tan Smiley (the youngest), and I attended the integrated Port St. Joe High School. Notably, the doors of George Washington School closed once federal mandates enforced school integration. Against the fading backdrop of segregation in Gulf County, schools would soon embrace these changes, although with some reluctance. A noted historical reference reminds us, *"For students who previously attended George Washington High School, these brave students weren't welcomed by all. Even though they had voluntarily enrolled in*

Port St. Joe High School, they were given limited access within the community and rode segregated buses," a student said during the program. " Black students were not allowed to be a part of some extracurricular activities, such as cheerleading, so they stayed the course and practiced peaceful protests, such as walkouts at sporting events and sit-ins on the grass in front of the school." The relentless courage of my predecessors, who faced these challenges with determination, laid the groundwork for me to attend school with peers who did not look like me. Even so, while the highest court in the land abolished the clause of separate but equal, the wheels of justice turned much slower in southern states, such as Florida. It would take a considerable journey before the dreams of activists and legal champions would come to fruition. However, in time, the barriers of discrimination that divided schoolchildren began to collapse.

Mr. Monette, a figure of respect and wisdom, often spoke of the issues teachers in the sixties and seventies faced during the transition period of integration. The Gulf County school district did not fully desegregate its schools until 1970. As Mr. Monette said, "There were many days of physical violence due to stereotypes held by both Blacks and whites," Yet, his presence and influence were a calming force, ensuring that the students' dignity or integrity stayed intact. He believed that the greatest accomplishment of integration was that by attending school together, students had the opportunity to confront unspoken biases towards people of different racial or ethnic backgrounds." Mr. Monette's role in promoting understanding and respect among students was crucial.

Port St. Joe High School was integrated in 1970 with the opening of a new building at its current location, leading to the closure of the segregated George Washington High School. Mr. Monette was transferred to Port St. Joe High from the all-Black Washington High School. He and other Black educators caringly shepherded Gulf County African American students into a racially inclusive world. The closing of Washington High School occurred two decades after the Supreme Court's decision in Brown v. Board of Education, which ushered in crucial political and social changes for African Americans in the South. When I was still in high school, I remember Mr. Monette telling me what he witnessed at the height of segregation in Port St. Joe. His detailed stories helped us understand the hardships of our past in light of what we looked forward to in the future. Although I may never be sure, Mr. Monette told his stories to heal the hurt of racism and discrimination while also giving us the courage to open the doors of greater possibilities. When integration was implemented in Gulf County, he thought it was his professional duty and obligation as a dedicated educator to teach all children regardless of race, ethnicity, or political stripes.

Teenage Years and Having a Job

Hard work, self-reliance, and independence were adherently practiced in our home. My parents modeled these meaningful virtues, mainly being gainfully employed, so I was eager to get a job and hold my own as a teen. My father worked the early shift at St. Joe Paper Company, and by 5:00 in the morning, he would have already been up and made his cup of Maxwell House Coffee on the stove before going to work. Even today, the aroma of freshly brewed coffee brings back memories of hearing him gathering his belongings as he said goodbye to my mother on his way out the door. My father took immense pride in his work at St. Joe Mill while raising a large family. And though the smell from the mill was offensive to visitors, residents had few problems with it because it was where they earned a good living.

The mill was a major employer for both Blacks and whites, contributing significantly to the local economy. With abundant pine trees in the surrounding areas, a reliable shipping outlet on the Gulf, and a dependable rail system, the mill was a cornerstone of the community. However, its closure in 1999 had a devastating effect, wiping out good-paying jobs and future employment opportunities for many.

Life was pretty good for me as an average fifteen-year-old. Typically, up and ready to go at 5:00 a.m. on weekend mornings, I would get on my 350cc red Honda motorcycle and head to the St. Joseph Bay Country Club. The Country

Club is about ten miles away by motorcycle from where I lived in North Port St Joe. As I leaned into winding curbs on Highway 98 towards work, I would ride my bike lying low to minimize the brisk, cool wind from the Gulf. I loved that bike; it was my relaxation. Once at the Club, I washed and cleaned twenty electric golf carts so members could start golfing around 8:00 in the morning. It would take a couple of hours to finish the job. After cleaning golf carts at the Club on the weekends, later in the morning, I joined my father for several hours in the wooded forest to go "baiting." My father operated a baiting business after retiring from St. Joe Paper Company. It was not unusual for him to take ten to fifteen young people and adults on his old rusty white F150 Ford truck to area woods in the early morning hours to engage in a process called "baiting." Baiting for profit has been lucrative commerce for generations in our region of Florida.

One of the first papers written in my first-year composition class at FSU in 1977 was on the process of baiting. Most people are unfamiliar with this age-old tradition, which involves driving a wooden stake into the ground and rubbing a piece of iron or brick on top of the wooden stake to create a vibration that causes earthworms to come out of the ground. We collected thousands of worms on each baiting excursion and sold them to wholesalers who sold them for use as freshwater fish bait. After collecting the "payroll" from the wholesaler, I was responsible for paying the workers. It was my first lesson in managing money. Workers could earn twenty-five or more dollars a morning baiting in the scruffy pine woods of Port St. Joe in the seventies. It was considered good money. I often earned enough money to get the things I needed without relying on my parents. I got a good taste of what it was like to be self-reliant, and I liked that mindset.

During the week, in my eleventh and twelfth-grade years, I worked as a custodian assistant after school for about two hours a day. Principal Edwin G. Williams hired me to clean the front of the high school and to help the custodial workers clean the classrooms. His trust in hiring me meant I had to take the job seriously and do my best. My job was both humbling and self-advising. Little did I realize then that in the future, I would fight to help people with meager means and of social or financial adversity by no fault of their own.

After finishing my custodial task during the week, I cleaned golf carts at the country club. It is hard to imagine now, but I held three jobs simultaneously as a teenager. I never remember not having the money to buy my clothes or being 'broke' as a teen. A few years ago, I found a pay stub from my job as a custodial assistant at Port St. Joe High School 47 years ago. My work then wasn't easy, but I learned that hard work and persistence were critical to achieving my goals.

Forty-five years later, one of the custodial staff I worked with, Mrs. Bessie Willis, requested that I deliver the Eulogy at her funeral. It was meaningful to know that I had made an impression of such magnitude on her. Likewise, I was honored when the school custodians, Deacon E.L. and Cile Fleming, Mrs. McArthur, Mrs. Alma Bryant, Ms. Queen Pittman, and Ms. Joyce Isaac, attended my attorney installation ceremony at the Port St. Joe Courthouse in 1985.

There were many good examples of putting pride into everything we did to garner trust and respect. One of my earliest business lessons came from observing Mrs. Gladys Stallworth at the local community grocery store she owned in the sixties. She precisely operated her manual cash register and counted money back to customers in a voice of respect. Somehow, this simple practice mattered not only to the customers but also to her. Life lessons and acquired skills that were critical to my success confirmed my parent's constant prayer that their children would benefit from educational opportunities.

College for anyone from Port St. Joe in the 60s and 70s was monumental, regardless of where they pursued a higher education. Most college-bound high school graduates went to Florida Memorial College in Miami, Edward Waters College in Jacksonville, or Florida A&M University in Tallahassee. As a teenager, I remember that a collection plate was routinely set out during church offerings for donations to Florida Memorial College. Founded in 1879 in Live Oak, Florida, the college relocated to the southern city of Opa Locka in Miami-Dade County in 1968. The famous "Negro National Anthem," *Lift Evey Voice and Sing*, was written by J. Rosamond Johnson, who taught at Florida Memorial College.

Despite being private institutions, participation in the Civil Rights movement was apparent at Edward Waters and Florida Memorial College. Students at both colleges protested segregation and racial injustices alongside their public counterparts by getting involved in sit-ins, wade-ins, and swim-ins inspired, in part, by the non-violent leadership of Dr. Martin Luther King, Jr. Yet, it was not until the late '60s and early '70s that Black students could enroll in large numbers at state universities in Florida.

Florida A&M University (FAMU) has always been part of the state's public university system. The university was established in 1887 as a state Normal College for Colored Students. The eighth President of FAMU, Dr. Frederick Humphries, was born on December 26, 1936, in Apalachicola, Florida, a small community 30 minutes from my home in Port St. Joe. He attended Holy Family Catholic School and the small, all-Black Wallace M. Quinn High School in Apalachicola.

Recently (July 2024), my high schoolmate, Dr. Tim Beard, was appointed interim President of FAMU, recognized as one of the nation's Historically Black Colleges and Universities (HBCUs). We were close neighbors in our youth, living blocks apart in North Port St. Joe. He is another example of how having good character and an excellent educational background laid the groundwork for his leadership at Florida A&M University.

In the late seventies, my life took a turn toward my highly anticipated future. I was bright-eyed and curious about what the world had to offer. The year was 1976. I started a journey that would influence my life beyond measure. I traveled from my hometown to Florida's capital city, Tallahassee, that summer to attend the Annual Florida American Legions Boys State Conference. The Gulf County American Legion sponsored my attendance at the prestigious conference. School Guidance Counselor Sarah Riley, American Legion members, and veterans L.C. Clark and Calvin Pryor, Sr., were instrumental in my selection to attend the Boys State Conference. Since its beginning in 1935, it has been recognized as one of the most highly acclaimed opportunities for rising 12th-grade boys. Naturally, I was proud to represent my community as American Legion chapters chose conference participants from their respective counties. Teen nominees are selected after meeting stringent qualifications, such as high academic standing and a morally good character. To have been judged in such a way and chosen from among so many others was gratifying.

As a young Black kid from a small rural town, the American Legion's Boys State and the Presidential Classroom programs were transformative for me. These unique experiences, which I had never encountered, exposed me to a world of people, places, and opportunities, igniting new and bigger dreams.

Boys State is a real-time simulation that mirrors the state of Florida government led by high school boys. The activities help the participants understand the interworking of state and local government. Additionally, teens are exposed to governmental and business leaders. The annual conference occurred at Florida State University during my participation in Boys State in 1976. I was recruited to attend FSU while at Boys State. I probably would not have attended FSU if I had not participated in such a rewarding Boys State experience at FSU. I developed what turned out to be a lifelong friendship with Jarvis Bracy from Kissimmee, Florida. I soon learned that the world was much bigger than I imagined when I arrived in Tallahassee. For me, there were many firsts. It was the first time I visited a college campus and the first time I had lived away from home for a week. It was also the first time I rode in an elevator in the FSU dormitory where Boys State participants lived. It was also the first time I developed an interest in pursuing a legal career. At Boys State, I first saw the doors of immense opportunities waiting to be opened. The Boys State conference gave me and the other boys a platform to model state government activities while learning and practicing leadership skills in the Halls of the Florida Government. Along with other Boys State members, I wrote bills, engaged in debates and mock trials, and ran for elected office. I served as an attorney and local government official at Boys State.

The 1977 Presidential Classroom for Young Americans was another event that inspired me to pursue my goals. This high school program is where selective students spend a week in Washington, DC, and experience an inside look at the nation's capital. It was my first time flying on an airplane and visiting Washington, D.C. The students listened to national government leaders and visited key government sites.

Supreme Court Justice Thurgood Marshall, Frank Fitz Simmon, President of Teamster Union, and Congressman Bob Sikes were among the officials who spoke to our class. I still have photos of these encounters after fifty years. I met Senator Lawton Chiles at the Presidential Classroom. Twenty years later, he appointed me as a Judge. We visited the White House and the Treasury Department, where currency/money is printed. There, too, I was introduced to awe-inspiring experiences. A crowning point of this conference was seeing Justice Thurgood Marshall, a Black Justice, in person. Hearing him speak to the wide-eyed group of Presidential Scholars participants made me incredibly proud. It isn't easy to quantify this experience's impact on my ability to dream of possibilities, but the sum of the Washington, D.C. experience was life-altering.

Chapter 4
COLLEGE YEARS 1977-1985: THE FSU EXPERIENCE

Undergraduate Years 1977 – 1981

Law School 1981-1985

"WOW! My undergraduate and law school student years at Florida State University were positive and rewarding. I learned a lot, which laid the groundwork for my memorable career."

TWO PRESIDENTS MEET-1979-FSU President Bernard Sliger greets Elijah Smiley, President of the Black Student Union, at The President's annual ice cream social on the lawn of Sliger's home.

When I arrived at Florida State University (FSU), post Boys State and the Presidential Classroom, Jimmy Carter was elected President of the United States. His election was an anomaly. When he took the oath of office, one would have hardly imagined that he, an obscure politician, and a man with such a humble spirit, would have become the President of the United States. Still, he believed in himself and thought he could achieve it. The path to becoming the leader of the most powerful country in the world started with a family of peanut farmers from Plains, Georgia. As I followed President Carter's presidency, I learned he led with kind and modest strength. His leadership from the Oval Office made memorable and enduring marks on me personally and in American society. He helped us see how someone from the smallest of communities could rise to the challenge of leading at home and abroad. President Carter's Camp David Accords and the Panama Canal Treaties were among his historic achievements. During Carter's presidency, I began to see the bigger picture of how to persist and reach my goals. Going off to college was the next step in my journey.

Arriving in Tallahassee in the 1970s was a journey filled with anticipation and excitement. The prospect of beginning college was highly anticipated. The thought of living independently in a new location away from home was also exciting. I would leave a familiar community to whom I owed tremendous debt. I would be putting my independence and self-reliance to the test, particularly since many good people had lifted me above the limits of our community to achieve remarkable things. Summer in Tallahassee was exactly as expected when we got there. It was boiling in the upper nineties, and the humidity was punishing. Once at the universi-ty, we eventually found our way to the dormitory where I would be living. Another phase in the journey of my life was about to begin.

I was amazed by how Tallahassee was many times bigger than Port St. Joe. Seven of its rolling red clay hills, as I eventually learned, dominated the land-locked landscape. These hills, along with the centuries-old oak trees, held secrets of a sometimes dark and checkered historical past; it was a landscape that was visibly different from where I grew up. The capital city had images of wealth and poverty alongside intermittent signs of economic progress. Black people and whites in the town cohabitated in disparate living conditions. It was a city divided into four distinct quadrants. Most of its poorest citizens lived in the southern quadrant, separated by railroad tracks, a typical southern town characterization.

A First-Generation College Student

My journey as a first-generation college student at Florida State University from 1977 to 1981 was a significant achievement. I was only the second person in my family to attend and graduate from college, following in the footsteps of my brother, Joseph, who is now the Dean of Social Science at St Petersburg College. This achievement filled me with a sense of pride and admiration for the opportunities that education had provided me.

WOW! My undergraduate and law school student years at Florida State University were positive, rewarding, and transformative. I learned a lot, which laid the groundwork for my memorable career. I am grateful to the university for the opportunities afforded to me. I arrived at the University at 17, with Kellum Hall being the tallest building I had ever seen. I departed the University in 1985 with a bachelor's degree in government and a Juris Doctorate. Between arrival and departure, I acquired vast knowledge, forged lifelong friendships, and developed a firm belief that everything was POSSIBLE. Buzzing with excitement and a view that most issues or problems could be analyzed from a legal, business, or moral perspective, my goal was to enhance my knowledge by pursuing government, business, and law degrees. I was hopeful about the possibilities for the future during my first year at FSU in 1977. There were so many new experiences for a kid coming from a small town of a few thousand people. Most of the classes had fewer than fifty students, but the lecture classes at Ruby Diamond Auditorium felt as if there were more students in the class than people in my hometown of Port St. Joe. I was lucky to live in DeGraff Hall, a small dormitory of about two hundred students. While there, I reunited with Jarvis Bracy, whom I had met at the American Legions Boys State, and Keith Blanden at the Progressive Missionary Baptist State Convention in 1976. We became lifelong friends. The communal living of a small dormitory provided the benefits of a tight-knit family where communicating and having a good relationship with others were critical skill sets. The annual soul food dinner at the dormitory was heartwarming and allowed the students to showcase their cooking skills. FSU Student Vice Presidents Dr. Bob Leach and Sherrill Ragans always attended the occasion. The students in DeGraff Hall genuinely cared for and supported each other. Most of the students, like me, were first-generation college students whose parents were not college graduates. College, a golden opportunity, was new and different for us, and our goal was to navigate it successfully. We studied like crazy to pass our classes, but more importantly, we learned about resilience, determination, and the power of community.

It was a monthly ritual for us to walk from our dormitory to Gilliam's Brothers Barbershop in the Historic Tallahassee Frenchtown. We received expert haircuts and gained wisdom not found in our schoolbooks from Reverend Ervin Gilliam, Sr., at the barbershop he established in 1966. He shared knowledge during our conversations while getting haircuts, blended life advice, historical insights, and personal anecdotes. The esteemed Justice Joseph Hatchett, whom I greatly admire, was also a patron of Gilliam's Barbershop. The Frenchtown area in Tallahassee was a thriving business hub for black-owned businesses in the 1960s and early 1970s. Gilliam Barbershop stands as one of the few remaining establishments from that era. This story represents the typical narrative of Black business hubs that thrived in communities across the South.

After successfully completing my first and second years, I became engaged in campus student politics.

Student Leadership and Advocacy

Student advocacy politics was exciting and provided a learning ground for developing organizational, negotiating, and interpersonal skills. I was involved in student advocacy politics on campus, state, and national levels, which included serving as President of the statewide Florida Black Student Association, Vice President of the National Black Law Student Association, and on the Executive Board of the American Bar Association Law Student Division. My initial foray into student advocacy politics began with seeking the FSU Black Student Union (BSU) leadership post, the leading student advocacy group in the seventies for black students. Our student campaign theme, "Unity, Professionalism, and Morality," reflected our desire to be role models and make positive changes. We emerged victorious in the closely contested 1978 Black Student Union (BSU) election. We embarked upon the most intense and productive agenda ever for the BSU, which included engaging FSU President Bernard Sliger, Vice President Dr. Bob Leach, and Administrator Dr. Freddie Groomes to secure additional Black counselors, a new BSU House, and the hiring of Dr. Ashenafi Kebedi as Cultural Center Director. During our years of student advocacy, we made significant progress, served as positive role models among our peers, and instilled a sense of morality and professionalism.

1980 FSU Student Leaders-President Elijah Smiley, Vice President Arthur Fleming, Treasurer Anthony Brighman, and Secretary Stephanie Fletcher

Statewide and National Student Advocacy

I dreamed even bigger and was elected President of the statewide student advocacy group, the Florida Black Students Association, in the early 1980s. While at the leadership helm of the FBSA, we developed the PACE STATEWIDE STUDENT PLAN for the eighties. The PACE PLAN comprised four interlocking components: **P**olitical, **A**cademic, **C**ultural, and **E**conomic. It was the first comprehensive statewide student plan that sought to capture and direct students' energy, aspirations, and idealism into improving our communities and effecting positive changes for students throughout Florida. An integral part of the Plan was to urge students to obtain the highest level of education and to return to their community to be positive role models for the betterment of their communities. The statewide association benefitted greatly from the wisdom and advice of a cadre of statewide faculty student advisors, including FAMU-Dr. Bill McCray, FSU-Dr. Naim Akbar, Gulf Coast State College Advisor-Leon Miller, St. Petersburg State College Advisor-Dr. Joseph Smiley, and FSU-Professor Dr. Bill Jones. Their guidance and support were invaluable in shaping the direction and impact of our advocacy work. Other long-time advisors included Donald Cleveland, Willie Felton, and Sabria Farrakhan, who also played significant roles in our journey.

The Law School Experience

My involvement in student government and campus politics fueled my desire to attend law school. When I was admitted to FSU Law School in February 1981, it was a moment of great pride and accomplishment. Many of my friends who were also student leaders, such as Mel Wilson(Attorney), Willard Proctor(Attorney), Arthur Fleming(Attorney), James Ruth(now a Duval County Judge), Michael Andrews(now a Florida Circuit Judge), and Don Robinson(Attorney), were also accepted into law school and went on to become successful attorneys. This shared success was a testament to our hard work and dedication, and a source of inspiration for our future endeavors.

Even though I graduated from FSU with an undergraduate degree, law school presented a completely different experience from my previous four years. I encountered unfamiliar legal concepts and language. I had never set foot in a courtroom or met a Black lawyer until I entered college. Growing up in a small town with parents who had limited education, legal concepts, theories, and the court system were not part of my upbringing or family discussions. I had little knowledge of the legal system and saw it as something to avoid. I felt like I was starting from behind the starting line, but I was determined to put in the effort to succeed in law school. Participating in the CLEO Summer Pre Law School-Institute at Mercer University in Macon, Georgia, gave me the added assurance I needed to approach unfamiliar subjects confidently. My first-year constitutional and criminal law classes were challenging, but I began to feel and relate the topics to real experiences.

After successfully completing law school, I interned with the Florida House of Representatives Criminal Justice Committee and the Leon County Attorney's Office. I also did voter registration for the AFL-CIO in rural areas of Leon County. These experiences further broadened my understanding of the law. I began to conceive plans to use my legal education to contribute to the community positively.

Graduating from law school was a far-reaching accomplishment for me, my family, and my community. Because so many people had inspired and helped me along the way, it felt more like a community accomplishment than a personal one when

I graduated. I am probably the first Black person from Port St. Joe to graduate from law school and go on to become a judge.

Earning a Juris Doctorate was only part of the goal; passing the bar exam is the ultimate goal for law students. I spent the summer of 1985 preparing for the bar exam. I did not have the money to take a bar exam preparation course, so I spent six weeks in my FSU Alumni Village Apartment studying night and day for the bar exam. The only person I saw was the mailman who occasionally stopped by while delivering mail, and we chatted about his military experiences. I traveled to Orlando in July 1985 to take the two-day law exam. Probably three hundred or more students from around the state and nation were sitting for the exam. Some students must take the exam multiple times to pass. The preparation and hard work that I put in that summer paid off. I passed the exam in the first sitting.

Memorable and Notable College Experiences and Events

While in my second year of undergraduate school at FSU, I was selected in 1978 to serve as a resident assistant at FSU DeGraff Hall during my second year at FSU. My primary job was to assist new students and to help the head resident assistant manage the dormitory. Many of the DeGraff dorm students attended church on Sundays. They probably attended church back home before starting their college career at the university. Keith Blanden, Jarvis Bracy, and I cemented our lifetime friendship during our college years at FSU. Our bond extended well beyond school; we attended each other's parents' funerals and were there when we married.

Tallahassee had quite a few prominent national fiery and eloquent preachers in the 70s and 80s. During our college years, we attended various churches in the community every week to hear these great preachers. Fortunately, these churches were within walking distance of the FSU campus on Tennessee Street and other streets nearby. These dynamic preachers included Rev. C.K. Steele, Rev. R.N. Gooden, Rev. Moses Miles, and Dr. Herbert Alexander. Hearing these influential and towering leaders speak about religious and justice issues was valuable and life-altering. Rev. C.K. Steele and the Southern Leadership Conference (SCLC) significantly moved our society toward a more accessible and just society. Despite his small stature, Rev. Steele embodied humility and kindness in a big way. I learned about his leadership involvement in SCLC with Dr. Joseph Lowery, Dr. Ralph Abernathy, and Dr. Martin Luther King, Jr.

National Leaders from the 1980s and 1990s

During my student years in the 1980s, I had the incredible opportunity to meet with many national leaders.

Muhammad Ali, nicknamed "the Greatest," is considered one of the most influential sports figures of the 20th century and is often hailed as the best heavyweight boxer of all time. He was the undisputed heavyweight champion from

1978 to 1979 during my undergraduate years. In 1999, the iconic boxing legend Muhammad Ali was honored with the title Sportsman of the Century by Sports Illustrated and the Sports Personality of the Century by the BBC. However, in 1967, Ali made a controversial decision to refuse military draft induction due to his sincere religious beliefs and his principled opposition to the Vietnam War. Consequently, he was convicted of draft evasion and had his boxing titles stripped. After a long and arduous legal battle, his conviction was ultimately overturned by the Supreme Court in 1971, sparing him from imprisonment. Meeting him in person was an absolute high point of my college experience. His sincere humility and quiet strength contradicted his public image.

Courageous Muhammad Ali-1979 visit to Tallahassee, Florida.
Elijah Smiley-FSU-BSU Student President, and Mel Wilson, Treasurer, Ray Gilley, Vice President

Rev. Dr. Joseph Lowery lived a full life dedicated to defending freedom and liberty for all people. He was a close confidant of Dr. Martin Luther King, Jr. In 1957, Dr. Lowery and Dr. King co-founded the Southern Christian Leadership Conference (SCLC), where he served as vice president.

Dr. Joseph Lowery & FSU Student Elijah Smiley-1979

When he visited FSU in 1979 for a speaking engagement,

I had the privilege of picking Dr. Lowery up at the airport and having a discussion with him as we traveled to the FSU student speaking engagement with extra security. Dr. Lowery also spoke at the funeral of Dr. King's wife, Coretta, and at President Barack Obama's inauguration in 2009. Dr. Lowery received the Presidential Medal of Freedom, the highest civilian honor. After his passing at 98, his legacy continued to inspire younger generations.

Reverend Jesse Louis Jackson, Sr., demonstrated exceptional academic achievements as an honor student and president of his student body at North Carolina A&T before immersing himself in the Civil Rights Movement. In 1965, in a pivotal moment, Jackson boldly decided to leave the seminary and join Dr. Martin Luther King, Jr., and the Southern Christian Leadership Conference (SCLC) in the historic march in Selma, Alabama. Throughout more than six decades, Reverend Jackson played a pivotal role in local, national, and international politics, tirelessly advocating for expanding economic opportunities and civil rights for all individuals. It was a profound honor for me to have the chance to meet Reverend Jackson during a visit to Chicago.

1980 Rev. Jesse Jackson, Rev. Tyrone Crider & Student leader Elijah Smiley

Chapter 5
LEGAL MILESTONES

"For thirty years, I have upheld my promise."

Judges of the Fourteenth Judicial Circuit, State of Florida in the year of 2000

Florida was organized as a territory of the United States from March 30, 1822, until March 3, 1845, when it was admitted to the Union as the State of Florida. At that time, almost half the state's population consisted of enslaved African Americans working on large cotton and sugar plantations between the Apalachicola and Suwannee Rivers in the north-central part of the state. As early as 1835, in North Florida, five or six large slave plantations were operating successfully along the Halifax River. Florida's Civil War Governor, John Milton, owned a large 2,600-acre- slave plantation in Jackson County, Florida, known as Sylvania Plantation, where cotton was grown, about eighty miles north of Port St. Joe, Florida. I have deep roots in Jackson County. My mother was born in Jackson County, and my grandparents are buried in Jackson County.

The Florida Legislature approved a secession ordinance, declaring Florida "a sovereign and independent nation." Protecting slavery was the reason for Florida's secession and the creation of the Confederacy. Even though the Emancipation Proclamation to end slavery was issued in 1863 by President Abraham Lincoln, the end of slavery was made formal by ratifying the Thirteenth Amendment in December 1865.

Florida's first constitutional convention occurred in 1838 in Port St. Joe, Florida, where I was born. Port St. Joe is known as the Constitutional City. A museum in Port St. Joe commemorates these events. When Florida became a State in 1845, The State Constitution provided that the Florida Supreme Court be composed of Circuit Court Trial Judges. The circuit judges were elected by the Legislature, collectively serving in the capacity of Justices of the Florida Supreme Court from 1846 until 1851. During this period, the state had four judicial circuits, which have since increased to twenty. The Florida court system now comprises seven Supreme Court Justices, 65 District Court Judges, 605 Circuit Judges, and 330 County Judges. Each of Florida's 67 counties constitutionally has at least one county judge. There are currently **six District Courts** of Appeal in Florida: Tallahassee, Tampa, Miami, West Palm Beach, Daytona Beach, and Lakeland. The **District Courts of Appeal** in Florida are intermediate appellate courts that provide the opportunity for thoughtful review of decisions of lower tribunals by multi-judge panels. District Courts correct harmful errors and ensure that decisions are consistent with established law, and their decisions most often represent the final appellate review of litigated cases.

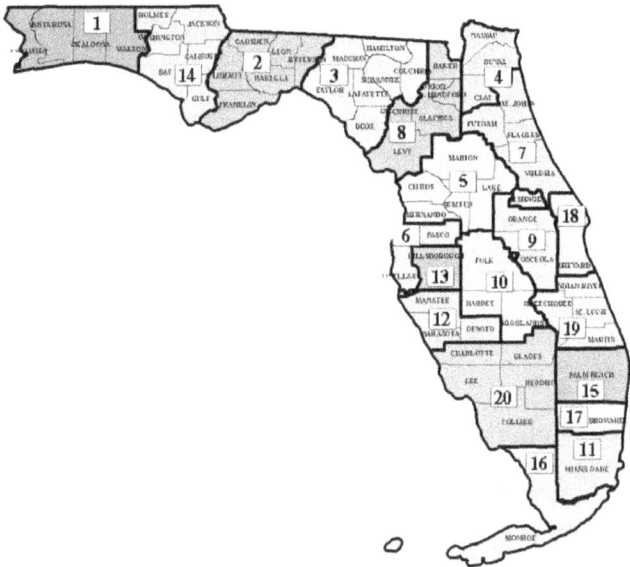

(Photo: Florida's State Court Judicial System)

As legal professionals, policymakers, and individuals interested in diversity and equity in the judiciary system, we play a crucial role in shaping the future of Florida's judiciary. With a population of over twenty-two million, it is vital that the judiciary reflects the rich diversity of our state. A well-qualified and diversified bench enhances the judiciary and strengthens our state. We acknowledge the significant progress made in recent years in diversifying the judiciary system, which is a testament to our collective efforts. However, there is still a need for more diversity, especially in the representation of Black Judges in Florida, both at the State District Courts of Appeal and the Federal District Courts.

Federal Legal Milestones

As legal barriers have fallen, the possibility of Black lawyers ascending to judgeships at all levels of our judiciaries has risen. Maine was the first state to admit a Black person, Macon Bolling Allen, to practice law in the mid-1800s. Twenty-four years after Macon Allen made history as the first Black lawyer in the nation, Dr. John Swett Rock achieved another milestone by becoming the first Black lawyer admitted to practice before the United States Supreme Court. Their groundbreaking and pioneering roles as two of the earliest Black lawyers to practice law in the United States carry immense historical significance, symbolizing the trailblazing efforts of Black legal professionals. Their achievements, overcoming significant challenges, paved the way for future generations.

Similarly, the remarkable achievement of Charlotte Ray, the first known Black woman lawyer in 1872, who earned a law degree from Howard University and passed the District of Columbia's bar exam, continues to inspire us today. Remarkably, Charlotte Ray was able to practice law before women gained the right to vote in 1920.

Judge William Hastie became the first Black Federal Judge in 1937 when President Franklin D. Roosevelt appointed him to the District Court of the Virgin Islands. In 1939, he became the Dean of Howard University's School of Law. One of his students was Thurgood Marshall, a lead counsel in one of the most consequential legal cases in U.S. history, Brown v. Board of Education. The appointment of Judge William Hastie as the first Black Federal Judge was a significant milestone in the judiciary's history. We owe great respect and appreciation to his pioneering role, which paved the way for future generations of Black judges.

Trailblazing **Judge Constance Baker Motley** was the first Black woman to argue a case before the United States Supreme Court. In 1966, President Lyndon Johnson appointed her to the Southern District Federal Court of New York, making her the first Black woman federal judge.

Possibilities for Black lawyers to participate in the judiciary at the highest level became a reality in 1967 when President Lyndon B. Johnson appointed prominent Civil Rights Attorney **Thurgood Marshall** to serve on The United States Supreme Court. Before his judicial service, he was an attorney who fought for Civil Rights, leading the NAACP Legal Defense and Educational Fund. Thurgood Marshall was a prominent figure in the movement to end racial segregation in American public schools. He won twenty-nine of the thirty-two civil rights cases he argued before the Supreme Court, culminating in the Court's landmark 1954 decision in Brown v. Board of Education, which rejected the separate but equal doctrine and held segregation in public education unconstitutional. His participation in numerous landmark Supreme Court cases involving Civil Rights, including Smith v. Allwright, Morgan v. Virginia, Shelley v. Kraemer, McLaurin v. Oklahoma State Regents, Sweatt v. Painter, Brown, and Cooper v. Aaron, underscored the importance of diverse representation in the legal profession and its profound impact on the judiciary system, highlighting the urgency of our role in advocating for diversity and equity.

Justice Katanji Jackson became the first Black woman to serve on the United States Supreme Court when she was appointed by President Joe Biden in 2022.

Judge Stephan Mickle is the first and only Black person to serve on the United States Northern Federal District Court of Florida. In 1979, he was appointed the first Black person to serve as a county and circuit court judge in Alachua County, Florida. In 2022, the Alachua County Criminal Courthouse in Gainesville, Florida, was named in his honor.

Florida Legal Milestones

The 1848 Florida Constitution was amended, and in 1851, authorizing acts were passed, providing that the Supreme Court should have its own Justices--a Chief Justice and two Associate Justices. The State Legislature elected these Justices for the term of their good behavior. In 1853, the constitution was amended to provide for the election of the Justices by the people for six-year terms. The 1861 Constitution provided for the appointment of the Justices by the Governor, with the advice and consent of the Senate, to serve for a six-year term. It would take over a hundred years for the first Black person to be appointed to the Florida Supreme Court. In 1975, Justice Joseph Hatchett was appointed to the Florida Supreme Court. Justice Peggy Quince became the first Black woman to serve on the Florida Supreme Court when Governors Lawton Chiles and Jeb Bush jointly appointed her in 1999.

James Dean holds a significant place in Florida's history. He was born in 1858 in Ocala, Florida, and is considered the first Black judge elected in the state. His pivotal election to the position of county judge in Monroe County in 1870 marked a noteworthy milestone in Florida's legal and social history.

The story of Black lawyers in Florida is one of struggle and triumph. During Reconstruction after the Civil War, many Black politicians and lawyers were able to improve their economic and professional plight. Among the earliest Black Lawyers to practice in Florida were Henry S. Harmon (1869), Joseph Lee (1873), Reuben Smith (1883), James D. Thompson (1874), Thomas de Saille Tucker (1883), and James W. Johnson (1897). The United States Census suggests that there was at least one Black female lawyer in Florida in 1940. Black lawyers were unable to attend Florida law schools until after World War II due to racial segregation laws. Despite the obstacles presented by the rise of Jim Crow Laws at the beginning of the twentieth century, these tenacious lawyers overcame adversity and succeeded in the legal profession.

Henry Harmon applied and was admitted to the Fifth Judicial Circuit in Alachua, Florida, on May 13, 1869, by Judge Jesse Goss.

Joseph Lee was admitted to practice law in Florida in 1873 after receiving his law degree from Howard University. Lee became a prominent Black Republican during the late nineteenth and early twentieth century. He served in the Florida House of Representatives from 1875 to 1888 and later became the first Black person to run for the lieutenant governorship in Florida in 1876. He went on to serve as a Jacksonville Municipal Judge in 1888.

James D. Thompson, admitted to practice law in Florida in 1874, joined forces with **Thomas de Saille Tucker,** who was admitted in 1884, to form the Tucker and Thompson Law Firm in Pensacola, Florida. The firm prospered in Florida and Louisiana with white and Black clients. A few years after Attorney Tucker set up shop in Pensacola, Florida, the State Normal College for Colored Students was established in Tallahassee, Florida, in 1887. Tucker left the practice of law to become the school's first president. Called the Florida Agricultural and Mechanical College for Negroes in 1909, the institution has been known as Florida Agricultural and Mechanical University since 1953. Tucker served as president until 1901 and is immortalized today with the building Tucker Hall, named in his honor.

James W. Johnson was admitted to practice law in Duval County, Florida, in 1897. Johnson is most famous for writing the famous Negro National Anthem, "Lift Every Voice and Sing."

Reuben Smith, born 1854, and **Armstrong Purdee**, born 1856, were from Jackson County, Florida, my mother's birthplace. Reuben was first exposed to law while working as an office boy in the law office of James C. McLean of Marianna. He graduated from Howard University and was admitted to practice law in 1883.

Armstrong Purdee was born into slavery on the Wardell Plantation in Jackson County, FL. His account of the Battle of Marianna was published in **The Kalendar**, the monthly publication of the Men's Club, St. Luke Episcopal Church, Marianna, FL, Vol. 1 No. 3, June 1, 1931. After slavery, Purdee, a protege of Florida State Senator William H. Milton, trained as a lawyer in Jackson County and became a successful businessman and an influential community leader. From the 1890s until the mid-1920s, Purdee published the *West Florida Bugle*, a Black newspaper.

Northwest Florida would not see its first Black judges until another hundred years had passed. They were Judge Ken Williams of the First Judicial Circuit in Escambia County and Judge Elijah Smiley of the Fourteenth Judicial Circuit in Bay County, Florida.

Virgil Hawkins never reaped the benefits of his personal sacrifice. He was admitted to the Florida Bar in 1977 when I graduated from High School. But there is more to this story. A preacher's son, Virgil, was born in 1907 and dreamed of becoming a lawyer. In 1949, at the age of forty-two, Hawkins and five other blacks were denied admission to the University of Florida because of their race. In 1950, the Florida Supreme Court ruled that Hawkins possessed "all the scholastic, moral, and other qualifications" of a successful law school applicant "except for race and color." He applied to law school again after the 1954 Brown v Board decision but was denied again by the University of Florida. Virgil Hawkins said, "I want to be a member of the Florida Bar when I die." Hawkins's dream of practicing law in Florida seemed to end, but it is POSSIBLE for justice to prevail. In November 1976, the Florida Supreme Court ruled 7-0 that Hawkins would be permitted to practice law in Florida. Hawkins died on February 11, 1988. In 2001, the University of Florida awarded Hawkins an honorary Doctor of Laws, the university's first posthumous honorary degree. The Florida Chap-

POSSIBLE

ter of the National Bar Association was renamed the Virgil Hawkins Florida Chapter of the National Bar Association. Dreams cannot be denied.

Sworn in as an Attorney

On October 25, 1985, the Gulf County Courtroom was filled with beaming eyes and overwhelming pride, not so much because of me but because attendees were able to witness through me a symbol that represented the realization of their aspirations, dreams, and hope. It had not happened before. Soon, I would become the first Black person sworn in as an attorney at the Gulf County Courthouse. Small deals for some can be big deals for others. How could it be? Can you be what you do not see? I needed to return home and be sworn in at the Gulf County Courthouse. I saw my first Black lawyer at the age of twenty at a barrister event at the law offices of Harold Knowles and J.R. Randolph in Tallahassee, Florida, after I began my studies at FSU. I had only seen a Black Judge from a distance as a part of a group of students in the Presidential Classroom listening to the United States Supreme Court Justice Thurgood Marshall. *Can you be what you don't see?*

Presiding at my swearing-in was the admired County Judge David Taunton, one of the few non-lawyer Judges in the State of Florida. A notable assembly of educators was present in the audience, comprising the esteemed Principal Edwin G. Williams, the knowledgeable Librarian Clarence Monette, dedicated Teachers Maxine Gant, Minnie Likely, Carl and Christine White, and Deborah Stallworth. I was especially thrilled to see my fourth-grade teacher, Ruth Phillips, among them. Packed in the Courtroom were a lot of people from our church, the community, and my family, including Deacon E.L. Fleming, Dorothy Daniels, Johnnie Best, Commissioner Alton Fennell, County Commissioner Nathan Peter, Jr., School Board Member David Sewell and State Representative and Attorney Billy Joe Rish. The custodial workers from the high school, Bessie Willis, Mrs. Cile Flemings, and Mrs. McArthur, were present, along with many seniors from the community. I was incredibly proud to see my beloved mom and cousin, Lula Bell Collins, there, too. Most of the seniors present were born in the 1920s and 30s and had never seen or interacted with a Black lawyer. They radiated with pride. The installation ceremony ended with a prayer from Reverend Otis Stallworth: *"Lord, thank you for this day. You've brought us a mighty long way. We are grateful for your grace and mercy. Thank you for the manifestation of our dreams. We pray that you bless our new attorney and grant wisdom. Amen."* These people believed in me. I had to make good on it.

Most problems can be analyzed from a legal, business, or moral perspective. I sought to advance my knowledge in each subject. After graduating from FSU Law School, I accepted a job as an attorney with Legal Services of Northwest Florida in Pensacola, Florida. While in Pensacola, I completed the Master of Business Administration program at the University of West Florida. In the 1980s, only a handful of Black lawyers were in Northwest Florida. Charles Wilson from Apalachicola, Florida, Nathaniel Dedmond, John Albritton, and Ken Williams were among the first Black lawyers practicing law in the Pensacola area post-1960. Governor Bob Graham appointed Ken Williams in 1985 as the first Black judge in the First Judicial Circuit, and Nathaniel Dedmond served as the first Black Assistant State Attorney in Pensacola. This was a significant milestone in the legal profession's history in Northwest Florida.

After serving as a staff attorney with West Florida Legal Services for two years, I applied for admission to Emory University's Candler School of Theology and the Interdenominational Theological Center (ITC) in Atlanta, Georgia, to pursue a Master of Divinity degree. I was all set to leave Pensacola to enroll at ITC in Atlanta in the fall of 1987 when Jack Mclean, Director of North Florida Legal Services, called and asked if I would head up the legal service office in Panama City, Florida. I accepted his offer with the expectation of attending ITC later.

When I arrived in Panama City in 1987, there were two black lawyers. Ted Bowers, born in Jackson County, was the first Black person to practice law in Bay County, and Quentin Broxton was the first Black Assistant State Attorney in Bay County. Cecile Scoon became the first Black Woman lawyer in Bay County when she was admitted into the Florida Bar in 1990.

I had heard of but had yet to meet long-time attorneys Ted Bowers, who was admitted to the Florida Bar in 1961, and Charles Wilson, who was admitted to the Florida Bar in 1951. Bowers and Wilson were instrumental in leading major desegregation cases in the Panhandle and Pensacola that integrated public schools and transportation in many Northwest Florida communities. For the few Black lawyers in Northwest Florida in the '60s and '70s, practicing law was risky. Bowers, in particular, endured many threats and humiliation in the 1960s.

After working as the managing attorney for North Florida Legal Services and the Public Defender's Office, I opened a successful private law office in 1989 on Harrison Avenue in Panama City, Florida. In 1990, I built a law office on Harmon Avenue in the Panama City Eastend Community. In the early 1950s and 1960s, the Eastend Community had several small, thriving Black businesses on Harmon Avenue, including Mama Coe's Restaurant, a boarding house, a barber shop, and a social club. These Eastend businesses only remain as memories and no longer exist. I made a personal commitment to the community by building my law office on Harmon Avenue, along with Dr. Michael Battle building a new dental office, hoping to rekindle the spirit of the Eastend Community.

Moreover, the greater Glenwood Community in Panama City has a rich history and had a thriving small business community in the 1950s, 1960s, and 1970s. The community had grocery stores, dry cleaners, funeral homes, motels, social clubs, and many beauty and barber shops, all of which contributed to the creation of many Black middle-class families and served as a source of wealth. I represented several of these business owners in the 1990s. These owners worked tirelessly to build and grow their businesses and create generational wealth. Unfortunately, most of these businesses did not have continuity plans and ceased operating after the owners' death. Very few thriving new small Black businesses in the greater Glenwood community have been created since the 1980s. My commitment to the community is unwavering, and I continue to work towards creating opportunities for growth and prosperity.

Call from the Governor to serve and the Promise.

I was at home on a sunny day for lunch on Friday, September 1, 1995, when the phone rang. It was Florida Governor Lawton Chiles on the line. He said, "Hello, this is Governor Chiles. Many people in Bay County support you, and my friends, Attorney Julian Bennett and Joe Chapman believe you would be a fair judge and do a good job." This call marked a significant turning point in my career, ultimately leading to my appointment as a judge. He added, "I will appoint you as the judge if you assure me that you will be fair, abide by the law, and serve the people well." At that moment, I recognized that my parents' prayers that their children would have opportunities they had never dreamed of had been answered.

I replied, "Yes, Mr. Governor, I promise."

For thirty years, I have upheld my promise.

The Official Installation Ceremony-The Investiture with Palpable Pride in the Air

At 1:00 on Friday, October 13, 1995, there was palpable pride in the air in the courtroom packed with friends, family, supporters, and local lawyers in attendance at my Investiture, the official installation ceremony.

An overflowing crowd of well-wishers and supporters gathered at the Courthouse to witness the 1995 swearing-in ceremony of the first Black Bay County Judge.

Many in the audience had played a role in helping and inspiring me along my journey. My father passed away during my second year in college. Thank God my mother was alive to witness this day. My first-grade teacher, Christine Williams, and other educators, Clarence Monette, Christine and Carl White, and Principal Edwin Williams, were in the audience. My long-time friend Keith Blanden was in the Courtroom. Visiting Judge Ken Williams, the first Black judge serving in Pensacola, Florida, and Judge James Ruth, one of the early Black judges to serve in Duval County, were in the jury box with other judges. It was the first time most people in the audience had interacted with judges who happened to be Black. The Governor does not usually attend the investiture of judges. Earlier in the day, we were surprised to receive a call that the Governor would attend the investiture. Governor Lawton Chiles presented me with my judicial commission during the ceremony, making me the first Black judge in the history of Bay County, Florida. Sitting in the front row of the Courtroom were Bishop Wiley McQueen, Educator Louella Washington, Panama City Commissioner Jonathan Wilson, and Callaway Commissioner George Smith, all of whom were born when Blacks did not fully enjoy the rights granted by the Constitution and for many, this day represented the realization of cherished dreams, full opportunity, and access for all people.

County Judging

It took about a month to close my private law office before fully assuming the judgeship seat held by long-time retiring County Judge Thomas Ellinor, who served admirably. Bay County had three county judges. I worked with long-time Judge William Cooper and Judge Tommy Welch to adjudicate the thousands of criminal, civil, and infraction cases filed in Bay County Court annually.

When Governor Lawton Chiles appointed me as a Bay County Judge in 1995, I became the first Black County Judge in the 14th Judicial Circuit, comprised of Bay, Gulf Calhoun, Washington, Jackson, and Holmes Counties. There are only a few Black lawyers in the 14th Judicial Circuit. I had to seek election in 1996 after my initial appointment in 1995 to maintain my position as judge. The election process was not easy, as many believed that a Black person could not prevail in a county-wide election in Bay County in the 1980s and 90s. Despite these challenges, I prevailed in the 1996 county judge election, a significant milestone in my career.

My tenure as a Bay County Judge, spanning 12 years from 1995 to 2006, and adjudicating over 30,000 cases as a county and circuit judge over the past 30 years, has provided me with a profound understanding of the legal system and the diverse issues before the court. As a County Judge, often known as "the People Judge," I have dealt with individuals directly, many of whom were not represented by a lawyer. This direct interaction with the individuals involved in the cases, often dealing with sensitive and personal matters, was one of the most challenging aspects of the role. Despite the challenges and pressures of the role, my dedication to justice has always been unwavering. I have consistently strived to be a neutral arbiter, applying the law to the facts of the case, even when it meant making rulings that I disagreed personally with but were mandated by the law.

During the early 2000s, Panama City Beach gained a reputation as the Spring Break Capital of the world, drawing in college students by the hundreds of thousands during April and May. The local County Judges were inundated with hundreds of cases every day during spring break, with most offenses involving underage drinking, disorderly conduct, and illicit drug possession. There were also some very serious cases. Witnessing the potential long-term impact of their actions, often driven by the excitement of spring break, was genuinely disheartening. These cases underscored the critical importance of making sound decisions. It's a reminder that individuals do not have the right to cause harm or damage to others or their property and that poor choices come with consequences. With profound empathy and understanding, I urge young people to consider their choices carefully.

Resigning to Run as Circuit Judge

Florida has two types of trial judges: circuit and county. Circuit Judges' jurisdiction extends to the most serious cases, including capital murder cases and other felonies. Trial Judges in Florida are elected Constitutional officers and stand for elections every six years. Florida's 'resign to run law' requires incumbents to resign their office if they seek another office while in office. I resigned as Bay County Judge in 2006 with no guarantee that I would win the race for the higher judicial office as circuit judge for the 14th Judicial Circuit. Seeking elective office in the 14th Judicial Circuit requires running in six counties: Bay, Gulf, Calhoun, Washington, Jackson, and Holmes. It is expensive and grueling because the circuit covers a large geographic area. No Black person had attempted to seek a circuit-wide elective position in the 14th Judicial Circuit. Every morning around 5:00 a.m., I was in the circuit greeting voters and workers as they changed shifts at hospitals, corrections facilities, restaurants, and industrial workplaces. Eddie Bell and Terrance Cotton joined me for weekend campaigning as we visited multiple counties, and a half dozen churches and organizations every weekend.

Although I was born and reared in Port St. Joe, the experience of campaigning throughout the six-county circuit enhanced my understanding of the people and places in the circuit. We participated in many festivals and parades, including the Watermelon Festival in Washington County, the Possum Festival in Wausau, The Pow-Wow Festival in Bay County, and the July 4th parades in Lynn Haven and Vernon. We held 'fish fries' in all six counties. I was told that a Black person could not win the six-county circuit-wide district, but I never doubted that I would prevail in the election. People are inherently decent and good. An elderly white gentleman whom I met on the roadside while campaigning in Jackson County confirmed this. He told me he had never voted for a Black person but would be voting for me. I also met a remarkable gentleman, Tamphus Messer, who introduced me to many of his friends in Bonifay, Florida. I won the circuit judges' election with significant support across the six-county area and overwhelming support from my hometown. I have successfully participated in six county and circuit judicial elections (1996, 2000, 2006, 2012, 2018, and 2024).

Circuit Judge Investiture-2006 and Circuit Judging

An investiture is an official public installation ceremony for a judge. Supporters and well-wishers from all six counties attended my investiture on December 29, 2006. This was a testament to the support and goodwill of the citizens of the 14th Judicial Circuit. Their active participation and well-wishes made this new milestone possible. I humbly accepted the great honor bestowed upon me by them.

Circuit Judges are called upon to hear the most complex and serious cases in our court system. They are invested with the power to make life-and-death decisions. Consequently, Circuit Judges are bound by a strict code of conduct. Circuit judges are prohibited from engaging in political partisan activities or presiding over cases involving a conflict of interest or where they cannot make a fair and unbiased decision. We must avoid doing anything that erodes citizens' faith in our court system, as this would ultimately weaken our democracy.

I have presided over thousands of circuit cases. Some cases are unforgettable. One such case involved the killing of an elderly veteran man. After his murder, he was placed in a deep freezer. The depravity of individuals can be astonishing. Even in cases like this, the judge must enforce the law while upholding the constitutional protections granted to all.

Chief Judging and Judicial Leadership

The Chief Judge is the chief administrative officer in each circuit and oversees its administrative supervision. The Chief Judge is elected by the other judges in the circuit. Very few Black Judges have served as chief circuit judges in Florida. I have been privileged to serve in every judicial capacity in the 14th Circuit: 12 years as county judge and 18 years as circuit judge, of which I served four years as chief circuit judge.

As the chief circuit judge, I worked closely with Judge Michael Overstreet, the counties in the circuit, and Senator George Gainer to facilitate the construction of a new courthouse in Washington County and an annex courthouse in Bay County. I also initiated the establishment of a veteran court, led efforts to create the Judge Larry Smith Award to recognize lawyers who displayed outstanding professionalism, and oversaw the implementation of an electronic case and warrant filing system.

Chapter 6
JUSTICE PREVAILS

"We hold these truths to be self-evident, that all men are created equal, that they are endowed by their Creator with certain unalienable Rights, that among these are Life, Liberty, and the pursuit of Happiness."

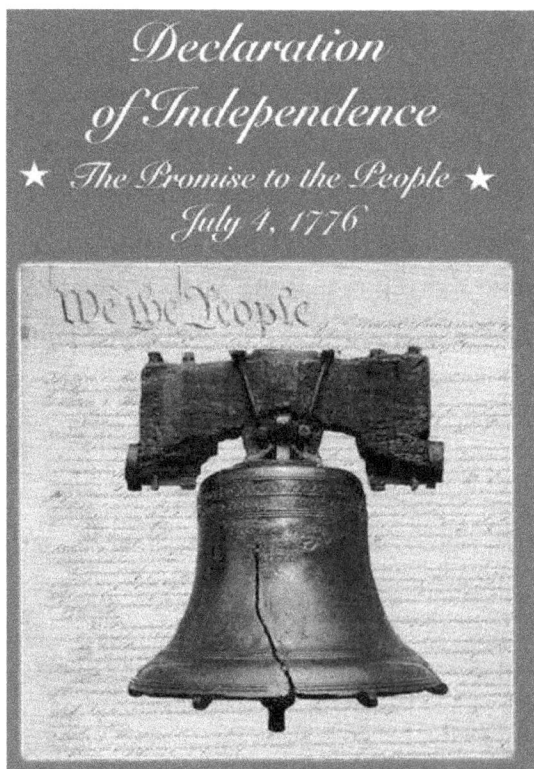

Theodore Parker, a Unitarian minister and prominent American Transcendentalist born in 1810, advocated for the abolition of slavery. He and Dr. Martin Luther King, Jr reminded us that the moral arc of the universe is long but bends toward justice. This idea expresses the belief that justice eventually prevails over injustice. Ohio, United States Congresswoman Shontel Brown points out that the moral arc does not bend towards justice on its own: "It only does so because people pull it towards justice. It is an active exercise, not a passive one." This underscores the power of individuals in shaping justice, empowering us to make a difference. Like mercy, the quality of justice cannot ultimately be constrained. People desire to be free. I believe that.

The **Magna Carta**, written in 1215 and known as the first written European Constitution, recognizes liberty and human rights.

The most famous clause of the **Magna Carta** states:

"No free man shall be seized, imprisoned, stripped of his rights or possessions, outlawed, exiled. Nor will we proceed with force against him except by the lawful judgment of his equals or by the law of the land. To no one will we sell to no one deny or delay right or justice."

The document established and codified many principles that still govern modern Western constitutional thought. The **Magna Carta**, with its direct influence on many common law fundamental documents, such as the Declaration of

Independence and the Constitution of the United States, is considered and recognized to be one of the most important documents in the history of democracy itself, as well as civil rights and obligations and common law in generally. The basic rights embodied in the Declaration of Human Rights, the Bill of Rights (1791), and the 14th Amendment (1868) can be traced to the Magna Carta, highlighting its enduring influence on the concept of justice.

The Principle expressed in the Preamble to the Declaration of Independence, "We *hold these truths to be self-evident, that all men are created equal, that they are endowed by their Creator with certain unalienable Rights, that among these are Life, Liberty and the pursuit of Happiness,*" has not just inspired Americans, but people around the world to fight for liberty and freedom. Its universal appeal transcends borders and cultures, igniting the spirit of justice and freedom in all who read it and inspiring us to strive for a more just world.

Dred Scott, his wife, Harriett, and their two daughters, like Homer Plessy and Oliver Brown, longed for the truths of life, liberty, and freedom. The Dred Scott v. Sandford, Plessy v. Ferguson, and Brown v. Board cases are the most significant legal cases impacting Black Americans' citizenship and human rights in American jurisprudence. These three cases serve as evidence that the moral arc of the universe bends toward justice.

The Dred Scott v. Sandford Case

Dred Scott, a man born into the cruel institution of slavery around 1799 in Virginia, endured a life of constant upheaval. He journeyed with his enslaver, Peter Blow, first to Alabama and then to Missouri, both slave states. In 1832, Dred Scott ventured with his second owner, Dr. John Emerson, to Illinois, a free state where the Missouri Compromise had outlawed slavery. After Dr. Emerson's passing in 1843, Dred Scott and his wife became the property of Dr. Emerson's wife, who returned to Missouri to live with her father, and she hired out Scott and his family. Despite her refusal to allow Dred Scott to purchase his freedom, in April 1846, Dred and his wife filed lawsuits in St. Louis Circuit Court seeking freedom under the "once free, always free doctrine." The Missouri law stated, " that any person taken to a free territory automatically became free and could not be re-enslaved upon returning to a slave state." Dred Scott, with a flicker of hope, believed it was possible for him to win his freedom since he had lived in a free state before returning to Missouri. The Courts ultimately did not deliver Dred Scott the justice he longed for. The United States Supreme Court ruled in the final majority opinion in *Dred Scott v. Sandford* that all people of African descent, free or enslaved, were not United States citizens and, therefore, had no right to sue in federal court and that the Fifth Amendment protected slave owner's rights because enslaved workers were their legal property. Dred Scott, along with several members of his family, was formally emancipated by his owner on May 26, 1857, just three months after the Supreme Court denied them their freedom in the Dred Scott decision. Scott died a free man at about fifty-nine on September 17, 1858.

The Plessy v. Ferguson Case

At the heart of the case that became *Plessy v. Ferguson* was a Louisiana law passed in 1890 mandating separate railway carriages for the white and colored races. It stipulated that all passenger railways had to provide these separate cars, which should be equal facilities. Homer Adolph Plessy, who described himself as "seven-eighths Caucasian and one-eighth African blood," challenged the Louisiana separate carriage law. On June 7, 1892, Plessy bought a ticket on a train from New Orleans bound for Covington, Louisiana, and took a vacant seat in a whites-only car. After refusing to leave the car at the conductor's insistence, he was arrested and jailed.

Convicted in a New Orleans court for violating the 1890 law, Plessy petitioned Judge Hon. John H. Ferguson, claiming the law violated the 14th Amendment's Equal Protection Clause. In the following years, segregation and the disempowerment of Black people increased in the South, and the North largely overlooked this. In 1892, Congress rejected a bill that would have provided federal protection for elections and invalidated certain Reconstruction laws.

On May 18, 1896, the Supreme Court delivered its verdict in Plessy v. Ferguson. The Court ruled that separate but equal facilities on intrastate railroads were constitutional and that the protections of the 14th Amendment applied only to political and civil rights, such as voting and jury service, not to "social rights" like sitting in the railroad car of your choice. In its ruling, the Court denied that segregated railroad cars for Black people were necessarily inferior. "We consider the underlying fallacy of [Plessy's] argument," Justice Henry Brown wrote, "to consist in the assumption that the enforced separation of the two races stamps the colored race with a badge of inferiority. If this be so, it is not by reason of anything found in the act, but solely because the colored race chooses to put that construction upon it."

The Plessy v. Ferguson verdict cemented the "separate but equal" doctrine as a constitutional basis for segregation, perpetuating the existence of the Jim Crow South for the next fifty years. Intrastate railroads were among the many segregated public facilities the verdict sanctioned. Other facilities included buses, hotels, theaters, swimming pools, and schools.

The Brown v Board Case

The National Association for the Advancement of Colored People (NAACP) played a crucial role in the fight against segregation laws in public schools, housing, and transportation. Their efforts led to the Supreme Court combining four related school segregation cases into one under Brown v. Board of Education of Topeka. By the time the Supreme Court considered the Brown v. Board case in 1954, Black Americans had endured sixty years of the "separate but equal doctrine" established by the 1896 Case, known as "Jim Crow" laws.

Thurgood Marshall, a key figure in the NAACP Legal Defense and Educational Fund, served as chief attorney in the Brown v Board Case. His personal journey, from leading the legal battle to becoming the first Black Supreme Court Justice thirteen years later, is a testament to the enduring struggle for civil rights.

Before the case of Brown v. Board of Education was heard, the justices were divided on how to rule on school segregation. Chief Justice Fred M. Vinson believed the Plessy verdict, establishing "separate but equal," should stand. In September 1953, before the case was decided, Vinson died, and President Dwight D. Eisenhower replaced him with Earl Warren, who was then the governor of California. It wasn't until the landmark case Brown v. Board of Education in 1954, at the beginning of the civil rights movement, that the majority of the Supreme Court essentially agreed with Justice Harlan's minority opinion in Plessy v. Ferguson that the "separate but equal doctrine" violated the constitution. In the majority opinion of the 1954 Brown v. Board case, Chief Justice Earl Warren stated that the doctrine of "separate but equal" had no place in public education. He called segregated schools "inherently unequal" and affirmed that the plaintiffs in the Brown case were deprived of the equal protection of the laws guaranteed by the 14th Amendment.

Justice evaded Dred Scott and Homer Plessy, while Oliver Brown and his daughter, Linda, eventually saw justice prevail, albeit after a long wait. The historical impact of the Dred Scott, Plessy, and Brown cases serves as a vivid testament to the enduring struggle for justice. Despite the often slow and arduous journey, these cases ultimately illustrate that the moral trajectory of the universe consistently moves toward justice.

Chapter 7
DIFFERENCE-MAKERS

*"Even after 40 years of serving my community as an attorney
and judge, I still hold these individuals in the highest esteem."*
February 9, 1998

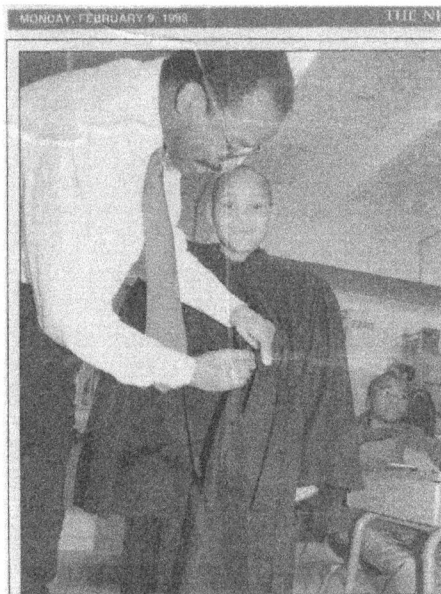

MONDAY, FEBRUARY 9, 1998   THE N[

Bay County Judge Elijah Smiley visited fourth- and fifth-grade students at
Millville Elementary School last week to encourage them to pursue their dreams.
Here he helps fourth-grader Micah Cherry try on his robe.

Judge visits awestruck students

TONY SIMMONS
Education Editor

There was no need to call the room to order
when Bay County Judge Elijah Smiley entered
Pequetia Freeman's combined fourth- and fifth-
grade class at Millville Elementary School last
week.

The children seemed almost awestruck as
they watched him pull on his robe.

Maybe that's because, prior to Smiley's arrival, Freeman talked with her students about
the work a judge does. According to the kids,

judges "tell people if they're guilty or not," and
they wear "long black robes and wigs" and
"bang a sledge hammer" to get people's attention.

Smiley helped clear up some of their miscon-
ceptions — at least the part about wearing a
wig. But mostly, he encouraged the children to
take their school years seriously.

"My father worked hard all his life. He had no
formal education. My mother had a third-grade
education. I am the first generation of my fam-

Please see JUDGE, 2C

Without realizing it, Difference-Makers can fundamentally touch the lives of many they never see through their actions and unselfish dedication to the community. Throughout my life, I have been positively impacted by Difference-Makers. Attorney Ted Bowers, Reverend C.K. Steele, Justice Joseph Hatchett, and Minnie Lucile Wynn-Williams are difference-makers who influenced my dedication to serving others. They faced incredible odds in their lives, yet through their unwavering perseverance, hard work, and bravery, they succeeded against all odds.

Air Force Veteran and Attorney Theodore "Ted" Bowers

Ted Bowers' father, born around the turn of the 20th century, had a vision for his children. He wanted one to become a doctor, another a lawyer, and the third a nurse. Ted Bowers and his siblings fulfilled their father's dream when he graduated from Howard University Law School in 1961 with an LL.B. degree. Bowers practiced law in Northwest Florida for over fifty years, including the challenging and perilous 60s and 70s for young Black lawyers. His father's dream was realized when Ted became a lawyer. Attorney Bowers was a Difference-Maker, not just a lawyer, but a beacon of hope for the hundreds of clients he represented. Many, including myself, admire his endurance, tenacity, and courage.

Reverend C. K. Steele, Sr.

Born in West Virginia, Reverend Charles Kenzie Steele (C.K. Steele), known as one of the nation's acclaimed Civil Rights champions, made his marks on history during the height of the Civil Rights Movement while living in Tallahassee, Florida. As Pastor of the Bethel Missionary Baptist Church, he was praised as a dynamic preacher, civil rights activist, and prominent Southern Leadership Conference (SCLC) member. He had a powerful presence in the pulpit, especially when reminding church members of the existential consequences of prejudice and discrimination impacting them daily. Under his spiritual leadership, the 1956 Tallahassee Bus Boycott was organized. The boycott, a testament to his resilience and determination, lasted for many months, sending a strong message to the local white leaders and demanding change. The boycott resulted in a substantial hit on the city's economy. Local economic impacts, along with the brilliance of the national limelight on Black voters' activism, ended the practice of segregated seating on city buses across the country.

Reverend Steele served as First Vice President of the SCLC under Dr. Martin Luther King, Jr. He also served as state and local president of the NAACP throughout the 1960s and 70s. He remained involved in efforts to eliminate racial discrimination in all public facilities across the South until he died in 1980. A statue honoring him stands in the public bus terminal, less than a mile from the church where he preached each

Sunday. Reverend C. K. Steele's legacy is ever-present in Tallahassee and the entire nation. Dr. Steele was small in stature but loomed large in moral excellence and humility. His steadfastness and determination to stand tall for justice influenced me from a distance. His activism was both inspiring and motivating. Sitting in the pews as a student and hearing him preach was awe-inspiring, uplifting, and energizing. His central message was that we all had a role in advancing freedom and justice for all people, including the "least of thee."

Justice Joseph Hatchett

Justice Joseph Woodrow Hatchett, a native of Clearwater, Florida, made history as the 65th Justice of the Florida Supreme Court. He was the first Black person appointed to the highest judicial bench since Reconstruction, a milestone that resonates in the annals of Florida's legal history. His tenure from 1975-1979 was a landmark, marked by his appointment by Florida Governor Reubin Askew. Justice Hatchett's journey began at Florida A&M University (FAMU) in Tallahassee, Florida, in 1954, the same year the Brown vs Board of Education case was decided. After a brief stint in the U. S. Army as a Second Lieutenant, he pursued his law degree at the Howard University School of Law, graduating in 1959, the year I was born. His path to the Florida Supreme Court was paved with numerous appointments as United States Attorney and United States Magistrate. His eventual appointment as Florida's first Black Supreme Court Justice was a testament to his resolute ambitions and undaunted purpose. It was in 1979 that President Jimmy Carter named him to the U.S. Fifth Circuit Court of Appeals, making him the first African American to serve in a federal circuit covering the Deep South.

Former American Bar Association (ABA) President Chesterfield Smith said, "Joe Hatchett exemplifies what is best in an American judge, one who is sometimes lonely, but one who never shirks standing alone." Such as it was, Justice Hatchett's ascent to the Florida Supreme Court was the result of resolute ambitions and undaunted purpose. Like so many others, he embraced a philosophy of hard work and good moral character. And because he had not been born into wealth, pursuing a well-rounded education required sacrifices and the constant support of caring individuals throughout his life. Though he never knew it until I told him in the rotunda of the Florida Supreme Court while attending an investiture ceremony, Justice Hatchett was not just a judge but a role model for me. His actions, dedication, and unwavering commitment to justice inspired me and many others. My aspirations to have a career in the legal system were partly kindled by how he represented himself as a judge and member of Florida's highest court and as Chief Judge of The United States Eleventh Circuit Court of Appeals. His presence on the bench of the Florida Supreme Court was beyond significant. It was apparent that he had diligently applied himself as a student, soldier, and lawyer and continually focused on goals that mattered. When he died, Judge Hatchett was honored with the Florida Supreme Court Lifetime Achievement Award in 2021.

Minnie Lucile Wynn-Williams

Minnie Lucile Wynn-Williams, a beacon of education, was born in 1918 in Apalachicola, a stone's throw from where I was born in Port St. Joe. Her children pursued higher education with her son, Ronald Williams, becoming a physics professor, and her daughter, Roselyn Williams, becoming a mathematics professor at Florida A&M University (FAMU). Mrs. Williams herself received her bachelor's and master's degrees from FAMU. She attended Paul Laurence Dunbar School in Apalachicola, Florida, where pioneering Attorney Charles Wilson also attended. Dunbar School was built in 1892 as the first school for Black Students in Apalachicola, Florida. She exhibited the highest examples of professionalism, excellence, and dedication to children's education. We all should appreciate and respect her unwavering dedication to education, her commitment to excellence, and her profound impact on the lives of hundreds of students. She served as principal at Bond Elementary School in Tallahassee and later as coordinator of Elementary Education for Leon County School District, Florida. The Smith-Williams Service Center in Tallahassee, Florida, was named in her honor. The Center provides numerous services for young children and seniors in the Bond Community. It wasn't until after I completed law school, when she visited my mother in Port St. Joe, Florida, with Cousin Lula Bell Collins from Apalachicola, that I learned about our family connection. Her father, George Henderson Wynn, born 1886, and my grandmother, Colorado Wynn, born 1887, were siblings. Her grandfather, Henry Clary Thomas, marched with General Sherman in the 103rd United States Regiment during the Civil War. Minnie Lucile Wynn-Willams was a Difference-Maker in the lives of hundreds of students.

Attorney Ted Bowers, Rev. C. K. Steele, Justice Joseph Hatchett, and Minnie Lucile Wynn-Williams, among others, continue to shape my decisions and actions. Their dedication, humility, and commitment to their respective fields have left an indelible mark on me. Even after 40 years of serving my community as an attorney and judge, I fervently hold these individuals in the highest esteem. Their influence is a testament to the lasting impact of positive role models.

Chapter 8
BE A DIFFERENCE MAKER: PUTTING THE SUCCESS PLEDGE INTO ACTION

There are no limitations on your imagination: Dream Big!

Do You Want To Be Successful?

That is, do you want to achieve your goals in life and enjoy the fulfillment of your dream? Success comes not by chance but by hard work and preparation. Sticking to the principles of the success pledge maximizes your chances of succeeding. The four critical components necessary to be successful are:

1. **Setting Clear Goals**

2. **Working Hard to Reach Your Goals**

3. **Making Good Choices Using Your Faith and Family Training as a Guide**

4. **Believing in Yourself and Never Giving Up!**

I. Setting Clear Goals: You must set clear goals and determine what is required to reach them. Embrace the transformative power of setting clear goals. It's not just about what you want to achieve but also about taking control of your destiny and shaping your future.

It is never too early or too late to set goals. Whether these goals are long-term or short-term, it is essential to have something to work towards and for shaping your future. Your dreams and desires may elude you if you do not have goals. You will have different goals at distinct stages in life. Some goals may be achievable in months, while others may take multiple years. New goals may be added as you accomplish your goals. Remember, it's okay to change your goals. This flexibility in goal setting empowers you, giving you the freedom to adapt and evolve, and allows you to stay focused and measure your progress.

Asking yourself the following questions will help you establish your goals and set you on the right path to success:

1. **What do I enjoy doing?**

2. **What do I do well?**

3. **What do I want to do to help myself, my family, and my community?**

4. **Where do I want to be in one year, five years? or ten years?**

Your honest responses to these questions will help you develop goals based on your natural skill set. It is best to pursue things you genuinely enjoy and want to do. After establishing your goals, you must determine the specific requirements for reaching your goals and the reasonable timeline to attain them. When I was much younger, I used a simple approach to achieving my goals: write them on a piece of paper and tape them on the closet door. Having it there made me see my goal statement every morning. The best thing about it was that it kept me focused on what mattered most in my future. You can, too. This simple approach works for individuals of all ages. After you accomplish your goals, you can add more to your list of ambitions.

II. Working hard and consistently to reach your Goals.

There is no substitute for hard work. Focus all your energy and talents on fulfilling every detail of your goals. Recognize that there are no shortcuts to succeeding. Don't just expect opportunities, like a job or degree, to arrive at your doorstep or in a text message. You must work hard and persistently to achieve the outcome you envision! Don't relegate yourself to a station in life that results from you doing less than your best. We are often encouraged to do our best and that you should never rest until your good is your better and your better is your best. Even if you fall short, re-evaluate, refocus, and remain determined to reach your goals. Someone said:

"If you can't be a star, be a moon. If you can't be a ten, be a nine. If you can't be a highway, be the best little trail leading to the hill. You win or fail, not by size, but by being the best at whatever you do."

This quote reminds us of the importance of putting forth our maximum effort to reach our goals.

As a judge, I often meet three types of individuals. Mr. Good, Mr. Fast, and Mr. Cheap. As you make decisions, remind yourself: If it is good and fast, it ain't cheap. If it is fast and cheap, it ain't good. If it's cheap and good, it ain't fast. So, if Mr. Fast, Mr. Good, and Mr. Cheap come around your neighborhood, tell them you ain't buying it because you believe in hard work. **Remember, success is not just about** the here and now; it's about playing for the long game. This is where true victory lies.

III. Good Choices Using Your Faith and Family Training as a Guide

You will be confronted with many choices. Bad or poor choices will hinder you from achieving your goals. Society imposes harsh consequences for some decisions you make. You should avoid making poor personal, family, and financial decisions with life-altering and long-term consequences that make it more difficult for you to accomplish your goals and the quality of life you imagined.

Personal Choices Matter.

A felony is any crime with a potential sentence of more than one year of imprisonment. The quickest way to relegate yourself to second-class citizenship and permanent underemployment is to get a serious felony conviction. The consequence of a felony conviction is real and gravely significant. For instance, an eighteen-year-old convicted of the possession of felony drugs, felony domestic battery, or grand theft of more than $300 will not be able to vote in most states, and his chances of obtaining a living wage job are substantially diminished. Most felons have difficulty obtaining a career in education, law enforcement, the military, the government, or the judicial system. That is a fact. Think about it. Without access to these career paths, many are left with minimum-wage jobs or risk getting caught up in the drug culture. You must avoid shackling yourself with the restrictions and consequences of a felony conviction by not participating in conduct that makes it possible.

Financial Choices Matter.

Most people desire a decent job that allows them to provide for their family, own a home, and accumulate some wealth to leave to their children. Understanding how the financial system has developed and how it impacts you is a powerful tool. Like it or not, a score is assigned to you--a credit score—and it is used to make judgments about you before you walk through the door of any financial institution. It is based on how you handle money and credit, your financial circumstances, and the decisions you make beginning at age eighteen. Your choices can cost you big! But armed with this knowledge, you can take control. You should know your credit score just like your social security number. Your credit scores range from 300 to 850, with a higher number being viewed more favorably. A credit score of less than 650 may preclude you from obtaining loans and a house mortgage, and if approved, you will pay a higher interest rate. Additionally, a lower credit score may prevent you from obtaining employment in some industries, renting an apartment, and securing insurance because landlords, merchants, and employers sometimes check applicants' credit history.

Even getting approval for a cell phone plan may depend on having good credit. Because bad financial decisions can be costly and drain your financial resources over time, seeking advice from people who have successfully managed their financial resources early on in your life is crucial. These mentors can provide invaluable guidance and support, helping you protect yourself from the adverse effects of bad financial choices.

Family Choices Matter

The 2022 data from the Centers for Disease Control suggests that the average lifespan for all Americans is 77.5 years and 72.8 years for Black Americans, with heart disease and cancer being the leading causes of death. Eighteen percent of Black Americans over the age of eighteen are in poor or bad health and 14 percent smoke cigarettes. You are most likely to develop the economic foundations for your life during your 20s, 30s, and 40s, with an opportunity to make real wealth progress in your 50s and 60s. A choice to have a child before you are ready, to develop the habit of smoking cigarettes or consuming unhealthy amounts of alcohol will get in the way of achieving health and financial prosperity. Cigarette smoking can have adverse health and economic effects on your overall quality of life. Cigarette smoking is the leading cause of preventable disease, disability, and death in the United States. The health effects of smoking on you and those exposed to second-hand smoke have been shown to increase the risk of cancer, heart disease, stroke, respiratory conditions, and even fertility problems. Cigarettes and unreasonable alcohol consumption can quickly drain several hundred dollars per month from your limited financial resources.

Too many young people in our community are limiting themselves by making poor choices, often dying from preventable causes. But you have the power to make sound personal, financial, and family choices. By making these choices, you take responsibility for your future and empower yourself to avoid the mistakes others have made. If you encounter a problematic situation and are unsure of what to do, reach out to someone in your family, community, or church whom you admire or who appears to have made the right choices or recovered from bad decisions. There are people in our history whose life story can serve as an inspiration. Strive to be like Jackie Robinson, who proved that ordinary people could do extraordinary things. Do not just be okay; strive to be like United States Supreme Court Justice Thurgood Marshall, a voice for justice. Don't just be common. Be like Barbara Jordan, who said long ago, "I can be president, too." Rise Above the Ordinary.

IV. Believe in Yourself and Never Give UP

There are no limitations on your imagination. Dream Big! No one has a monopoly on success. You can succeed despite your life station, your economic situation, or your family circumstances. Success is doing your very best to achieve your goals. Whether you do your best or give up is within your control. Only you determine whether you are successful. Even if you find yourself in a situation where the odds are against you (if you listen to the oddsmakers, you were not supposed to be here), your grit and determination make all the difference. I am betting on you. Never, Never, Never Give Up.

IF YOU FALL DOWN 5 times, GET UP 6 times.

IF YOU FALL DOWN 6 times, GET UP 7 TIMES

NEVER, NEVER GIVE UP!

Completing the success pledge and goal-setting form that follows will help you understand the four components of the success pledge *(setting clear goals, working hard to reach your goal, making good choices, believing in yourself, and never giving up)* and identify the requirements of your goals. President Obama once said, "If the world's going to get better, it's going to be up to you." I believe that latching your goals and ambitions onto this message from the first African American, twice-elected president of the United States, will help you achieve your aspirations and goals.

R.L. Sharpe suggests in his poem "A Bag of Tools" that each person has the power to create obstacles or opportunities with the tools they are given. I believe that. The poem says:

Isn't it strange
That princes and kings,
And clowns that caper
In sawdust rings,
And common people
Like you and me
Are builders for eternity?

Each is given a bag of tools,
A shapeless mass,
A book of rules.
And each must make—
Ere life is flown—
A stumbling block
Or a steppingstone.

I urge you to use your tools as steppingstones to success. It is your time to soar.

GOAL SETTING PLAN

1. Set Specific Goals

2. Understand the Necessary

Requirements to Reach Your Goals

3. Create a Timeline for Fulfilling each

Requirement Needed to Achieve Your

Goals

It is not a tragedy to fail to achieve your goals,
it is a tragedy not to have goals

THE END NOTES-THE AUTHOR'S FINAL THOUGHTS

"Thank You for the opportunity to serve the Citizens of the Fourteenth Judicial Circuit in Bay, Gulf, Calhoun, Washington, Jackson, and Holmes Counties for Thirty Years."

Judge Elijah Smiley

"Though I speak with the tongues of men and of angels, but have not love, I have become as sounding brass or a clanging cymbal."

We have celebrated over 248 years of sovereignty in this great country, and the opportunities enjoyed in Gulf County today were not so easily obtained. History has shown that pursuing human liberties- some occurring with sparks of protest and nationwide divisiveness—has sustained us as a unified country and brought us to where we are today.

Despite racial disenfranchisement, the Black community in Port St. Joe demonstrated remarkable resilience. Their dreams and ambitions shone brightest during the most challenging times. They found inspiration in those who showed unwavering tenacity to persevere against all odds, just like their white counterparts. This is why it's essential for us, as a community, to learn from our past. Our history is a rich tapestry of experiences, both triumphs and tribulations, which can enlighten us and guide our future decisions. Understanding our history allows us to make informed decisions, leading to a brighter future. It is not just a matter of knowing our past but learning from it to shape a better future for ourselves and our community.

Dreams are not just figments of our imagination; they are powerful tools that empower us to see beyond our circumstances, challenges, and perceived obstacles. The inherent power of our dreams cannot be denied or taken away. They are ours to make real, tangible, and true. I, too, envisioned fulfilling those dreams when I washed golf carts at the St. Joseph Bay Country Club, grunted worms to sell, or delivered a church speech as a youngster. Growing up, I never believed that I could not accomplish my goals or fulfill my dreams despite the external, legal, and societal limitations of the 1960s in rural Florida. The ability to aspire and dream is potent, and I firmly believe in that. You, too, have the power to fulfill your goals instead of just wishing for them. You have the power to put determined effort into reaching your dreams and desires. By the time I earned my undergraduate degree, I had envisioned my next important goals and was ready to work hard to realize them. I was prepared for the next step in my journey. I have tried my best to rise to the levels of wisdom and humility and the qualities of the Reverend C.P. Price, Reverend C.K. Steele, Educator Minnie Lucile Wynn-Willams, Attorney Ted Bowers, Justice Joseph Hatchett, and others. Today, many people with an array of talents, experiences, and knowledge can be helpful to those who are persistent and deliberate in their desire to learn from them.

Wisdom and humility are not bestowed upon us because of our status or wealth; they are earned through hard-lived efforts, humbling experiences, and the lessons learned from the outstanding people we meet over time. Humility, in its purest form, is a God-given gift. Therefore, we must commit ourselves to being humble, keeping an open mind, and being willing to listen and learn from the trials, tribulations, and triumphs of others. But we must also remember that we are not alone in this journey. Our community, with its array of talents, experiences, and knowledge, is here to help us. This is the path to true wisdom, and it is a path we walk together.

For close to sixty years, I have experienced an enormously blessed life. I have used my imagination and dreamed what was once unimaginable. You, too, can seize the opportunity to pursue your dreams and make them a reality. Adhering to the success pledge has allowed me to achieve all my major goals. Although I may not be able to do what you can do-*whether large or small*- I will do what I can to make my community a better place. I pledge to spend the rest of my blessed life striving for a positive impact on the world. It does not take much to be a blessing to someone.

They said, "That's Ms. Pecola's boy. She just went to grade school."

They said, "That's Mr. Joe's boy. He did not go to school because he had to work."

But I said, "It doesn't take much to make a positive difference." It is POSSIBLE. God has given us the gifts of hope, charity, and love. Be a positive Difference-Maker in your community.

The pioneers who paved the way for us deserve our heartfelt gratitude. Macon Allen became the first African American lawyer to practice law in the United States in 1844. Henry S. Harmon (1869), Joseph Lee (1873), and James W. Johnson (1897) were among the earliest Black lawyers admitted to the Florida Bar. John Rock (1865) achieved the historic milestone of being the first Black lawyer to gain admission to practice before the United States Supreme Court. Judge James Dean made history as the first Black elected judge in Florida, while Justice Joseph Hatchett became the first Black Florida Supreme Court Justice. Justice Peggy Quince broke barriers as the first Black woman to serve as a Florida Supreme Court Justice. Judge William Hastie was the first Black federal judge, and Judge Constance Motley achieved the same milestone as the first Black woman federal judge. Their tireless efforts and achievements are an enduring reminder that: *"A Charge to keep we have, A God to Glorify... To Serve the Present Age, My calling to fulfill; Oh, may all my power engage to do my Master's will..."*

Thank you to those who sacrificed, cried, and died so we may arrive at this hour of unparalleled freedom and opportunity. Thank you for letting me stand on your devoutly strong shoulders.

To the younger generation, I remind you of the old song that says,

"Your valleys may get deep, but hold on.

Your mountains may get high, but hold on.

Troubles don't last always.

Weeping and wailing don't last always.

God can make a way out of no way.

God can open closed doors."

You can accomplish your goals.

I have tried to serve the citizens with Integrity and Honor.

ABOUT THE AUTHOR

JUDGE ELIJAH SMILEY

Judge Elijah Smiley has served as a Florida Trial Court Judge for thirty years, including as a County, Circuit, and Chief Judge. He has adjudicated more than 30,000 cases.

Born, raised, and educated in Gulf County. Judge Smiley graduated with honors from Port St. Joe High School. Judge Smiley and his wife, Kathy, have one child, Danielle. Currently, he presides in the civil and probate divisions.

Judge Smiley believes education and training are the gateway to opportunity and economic success. He encourages all young people to take advantage of available education and training opportunities.

Judge Smiley holds a Bachelor of Science in Government and a Juris Doctorate from Florida State University. He graduated cum laude from the accounting program at Florida State University. He is also a Certified Public Accountant with a Master of Business Administration degree from the University of West Florida.

Judge Smiley has been a member of the Florida Bar for 40 years.

SOURCES AND REFERENCES

Brown v. Board of Education of Topeka, 347 U.S. 483 (1954).

Brown, C. S. (1959). The Genesis of the Negro Lawyer in New England. *Negro History Bulletin*, 22(8), 171–177. http://www.jstor.org/stable/44215547

CDC, National Center for Health Statistics.

Dred Scott v. Sandford, 1856 U.S. LEXIS 472 (1857).

Dunn, M. (2016). *The History of Florida: Through Black Eyes*. North Charleston, SC: CreateSpace Independent Publishing Platform.

Florida's First Black Lawyers, 1869-1979. (n.d.). Virgil Hawkins Florida Chapter National Bar Association.

History.com.

Jr, Smith, J. C. (1993). *Emancipation: The Making of a Black Lawyer, 1844-1944*.

Plessy v. Ferguson, 163 U.S. 537 (1896).

Styles, F.L. (1933). Negroes and the Law. The Christopher Publishing House.

The Constitutional Convention Museum, Port St. Joe, Florida.

The George Washington High School Museum, Port St. Joe, Florida.

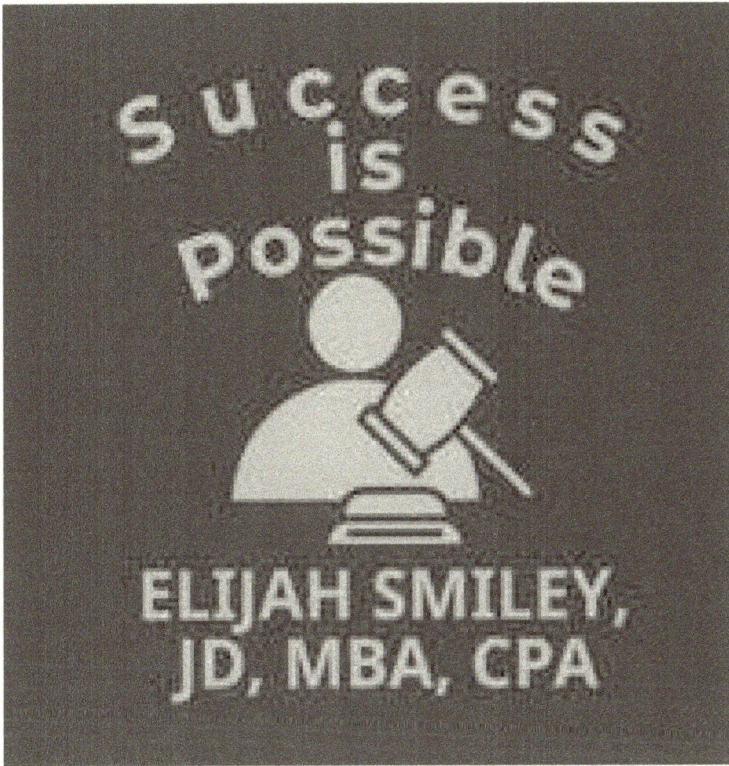

"Your feedback is important to us and to other potential readers. If you've enjoyed the book, please consider leaving a review on the website or platform where you made the purchase. I appreciate your consideration!"

elijahsmiley.com

smiley@elijahsmiley.com